About the Authors

Paul Dederick, right, and Bill Waiser.
PHOTO BY KARIN MELBERG SCHWIER

Paul Dederick is a prairie-born, CBC television producer based in Regina. After stints as a truck driver, potash miner, painter, bingo caller, and commercial radio sales representative, he was drawn to the field of journalism by his passion for writing. Paul has created many compelling television documentaries. He counts the *Looking Back* series as a highlight of his career and his friendship with his co-author, a highlight of his life. Paul's work has appeared on the *National, Venture, Country Canada,* and *Newsworld,* and he has received several regional and national awards. He is active in competitive sports, including touch football, volleyball, and golf.

Bill Waiser had no experience in television when he was invited by Paul Dederick to work on a pilot for a weekly Saskatchewan history segment for the regional news program. It was the first of forty-eight episodes and the beginning of a successful partnership and valued friendship. Bill is a history professor at the University of Saskatchewan and the author of several books, including the popular *Park Prisoners: The Untold Story of Western Canada's National Parks,* and *All Hell Can't Stop Us: The On-to-Ottawa Trek and Regina Riot.* When not teaching or writing, he is a recreational runner. He also likes to garden and canoe.

To Shona, for all that we've been through
and Ali, for all that is yet to come
P.D.
For Marley, Jess, Mike, and Kate
my toughest critics, my biggest fans
B.W.

Looking Back

TRUE TALES FROM SASKATCHEWAN'S PAST

Paul Dederick
Bill Waiser

FIFTH
HOUSE

Cover and interior design by John Luckhurst / GDL
Edited by Meaghan Craven
Copyedited by Alex Rettie
Proofread by Joan Tetrault
Photo credits on p. 121 constitute an extension of this copyright page

The publisher gratefully acknowledges the support of The Canada Council for the Arts and the Department of Canadian Heritage. We acknowledge the financial support of the Government of Canada through the Book Publishing Industry Development Program (BPIDP) for our publishing activities.

THE CANADA COUNCIL | LE CONSEIL DES ARTS
FOR THE ARTS | DU CANADA
SINCE 1957 | DEPUIS 1957

Printed in Canada by Transcontinental Printing

03 04 05 06 07/ 5 4 3 2 1

First published in the United States in 2003

National Library of Canada Cataloguing in Publication Data

Dederick, Paul, 1961-
Looking back : true tales from Saskatchewan's past / Paul Dederick, Bill Waiser.

Includes bibliographical references and index.
ISBN 1-894856-16-3

1. Saskatchewan—History—Anecdotes. 2.
Saskatchewan—Biography—Anecdotes. I. Waiser, W. A. II. Title.
FC3511.8.D42 2003   971.24   C2003-910367-6
F1071.6.D42 2000

FIFTH HOUSE LTD.   FITZHENRY & WHITESIDE
A Fitzhenry & Whiteside Company   121 Harvard Avenue, Suite 2
1511-1800 4 St. SW   Allston, MA 02134
Calgary, Alberta, Canada
T2S 2S5

1-800-387-9776
www.fitzhenry.ca

Contents

Introduction

LOOKING BACK ORIGINATED AS A SASKATCHEWAN PRODUCTION of the Canadian Broadcasting Corporation (CBC). Created and produced by Paul Dederick of CBC Television in Saskatoon, and researched and hosted by University of Saskatchewan history professor Bill Waiser, the series was broadcast weekly on the regional supper-hour news. The CBC aired forty-eight episodes between February 1999 and December 2001 and several were run on CBC Newsworld and other CBC regional shows. The episodes "The Blizzard of '47" and "The Price of Pride" received honourable mentions at the prestigious Columbus International Film and Video Festival.

This print version of *Looking Back* uses the same formula that made the television series such an overwhelming success. The collection examines compelling, little-known, often bizarre, stories from Saskatchewan's past. From the tragic to the light-hearted, the stories celebrate Saskatchewan, focus on real people, and—more often than not—feature a strange twist or kicker. Many also include the voices of people who had some special or personal connection to the stories.

These stories, like those presented in the series, are not intended to offer an in-depth analysis of historical players and events. Instead, they are written in a popular style for a general audience. They offer an appetizer, not a meal. Hopefully, readers will not only be intrigued by Saskatchewan's rich and varied past, but will want to learn more; a suggested reading list is provided at the back of the book.

The authors would like to thank several people who were involved in the *Looking Back* television series. Former CBC Saskatchewan executive producer John Brazill embraced the series concept from the beginning and insisted that it be a high-quality production, despite staff cuts, an extremely limited budget, and a weekly deadline. Former CBC reporter Amy Jo Ehman produced several episodes in her usual professional and skilful manner. A team of camera operators, editors, and journalists worked to ensure that *Looking Back* went beyond traditional "history on television."

Dozens of people suggested story ideas, gave interviews, or helped on location in a variety of ways. A number of institutions, in particular the Saskatchewan Archives Board, the Saskatoon Public Library Local History Room, the Western Development Museum, and the University of Saskatchewan Archives and Special Collections, kindly provided photographs and other visual materials for the show. A University of Saskatchewan Publications Fund grant provided money for the reproduction of the photographs in this book.

Finally, Fraser Seely, former publisher of Fifth House Ltd., first pushed the idea of turning the television series into a book—something that was keenly pursued by his successor, Charlene Dobmeier. What follows is our attempt to meet that challenge and, in doing so, promote a better understanding and appreciation of Saskatchewan's colourful history.

Locations referred to in *Looking Back*

The French counts formed a band at Whitewood.
SASKATCHEWAN ARCHIVES BOARD R-B 12483

The French Counts of Whitewood

~

IN THE LATE 1880s, A GROUP OF ARISTOCRATS LEFT FRANCE WITH grandiose dreams of building homes and businesses in—of all places—Whitewood, Saskatchewan. They came to Saskatchewan with their money, their servants, and their extravagant lifestyles. But the only evidence left of this extraordinary period in the province's history are the broken-down remains of once magnificent homes.

France's aristocracy was a threatened group in the late 1880s. The country had become a republic and the aristocrats were losing their preferred place in society. Many decided the Canadian North-West was the place to go. At least thirteen French counts came to Whitewood on the Canadian Pacific main line in present-day south-eastern Saskatchewan in 1885. Suddenly, the area could boast more nobility than any other place in North America.

The upper crust of French society introduced horse racing, classical music, and ballroom dancing to their bewildered neighbours. They would often rent the hotel in Whitewood and take it over for their extravagant parties. They also had ambitious plans to build thriving businesses. For the most part, however, their ignorance and arrogance would get in the way of success.

Count Yves de Roffignac tried to set up a sugar beet plantation complete with a distillery. The beets grew well. Everything was fine until he learned that distilling alcohol on a farm was illegal in the North-West Territories. Alphonse de Seyselle set up a cheese factory only to discover the acidic feed his dairy cows were grazing made for a very sour-tasting Gruyère. And then there was Maxim de Quercize. His sheep farm was running smoothly until his chief herder was killed in a horse-and-cart accident. No one else on the farm was skilled in raising and managing the livestock, so the operation soon failed.

There were some success stories. Joseph de Langle, for example, could not make a go of breeding horses, so he and his wife opened a general store in Whitewood. The people in town eventually warmed up to the French couple and the store prospered. But like many other settlers at the time, most of the counts were defeated by what must have been a strange and unforgiving place. Most of their ventures failed miserably, and by 1900 almost of all of them had abandoned their homes and businesses and returned to France.

Some Whitewood residents say the counts were arrogant, over-confident that their money could buy them success at any venture. Others say their failures resulted from a combination of circumstances and bad luck. Bernadette Gatin, however, blames it on their laziness. She is in her eighties and still lives in Whitewood. Her family moved to the area shortly after the aristocracy had vacated it. "They were counts," she says. "They had never worked a day in their life. Those guys had never worked. They didn't know what it was." Gatin has heard the stories of the aristocrats' extravagance. She believes that was what led to their downfall. "They rode horseback, rode the hounds. They danced. They visited. But they didn't work. They probably had a good time, but they all went bankrupt."

Despite their failings, the aristocracy contributed a colourful legacy of class and sophistication to the history of the Whitewood area, and one more important thing: their servants. Many of the families living in the area today are descendants of the people who originally came over as hired help for the French counts and decided to stay after their bosses had given up.

The Missing Recipe

⤳

THE GREAT DEPRESSION OF THE 1930s HELD SASKATCHEWAN IN ITS grip for ten long years. Windstorms blew in, drying up the prairie soil. Hard times also blew in, drying up the jobs. With no money and no crops, many people had trouble finding enough to eat. During this period, the railway served as a lifeline for prairie people. Relief trains sent from the East rolled in with much-needed supplies. They were filled with potatoes, apples, vegetables—and something else. Something no one on the receiving end could ever quite figure out.

Gordon Mcleod was raised on a farm near Elfros. He remembers struggling to get enough food for himself and his five brothers. "If we didn't have food at the table," he says, "we'd chip in from the neighbours. Everyone was helping each other out. We were pretty close-knit neighbours back then and every family helped the other out."

But neighbours were not the only ones helping out. People from the opposite end of the country did their part too. The fishing towns and villages of the Maritimes loaded prairie-bound relief trains with whatever they had. And what they had was cod.

Art Vessey grew up on the East Coast. He remembers how salt cod was a staple of his family's diet. "I thought it was great. I really enjoyed it," he recalls. "A favourite meal of ours was salt cod, turnips, and new potatoes. You couldn't beat it."

The fish equivalent of beef jerky, salt cod is hard as rock and grey as ash, and when it gets wet, it stinks like, well, old fish! It was flattened and dried so the pieces could be easily stacked and shipped. They were shaped like tennis rackets. The shape of the dried fish and the heavy salting it underwent meant it travelled well. The Canadian Pacific and Canadian National Railways waived freight charges on relief trains carrying food and clothing, so the cod was loaded in boxcars and sent to Saskatchewan.

Saskatchewan residents did not know what to make of it. "When I first saw the codfish," says Gordon Mcleod, "I wasn't too sure really what it was." Mcleod used to hitch up the family horse and wagon

Relief trains, sponsored by the Red Cross, carried much-needed food and supplies to Saskatchewan during the Depression. SASKATCHEWAN ARCHIVES BOARD R-A 15109

and ride into town with his father when the relief trains arrived in Elfros. "They would phone out from town and tell people that the boxcar was coming in. And everybody would come in with flour bags and stuff and fill a couple of bags. And I just forget how much codfish we got."

Mcleod's mother didn't have a clue what to do with the strange stuff her husband and son brought home. "She finally figured out to soak it in milk overnight and fry it the next day for dinner or bake it," Mcleod says.

Art Vessey says there is only one way to cook salt cod: soak it, simmer it and eat it. "It seems so simple to me how to cook it. But they did all kinds of weird things with salt cod. I've heard boil the blazes out of it and all kinds of things—weird things. It's a very simple thing to make." But it was not so simple for the thousands of prairie people who received this seafood delicacy. They tried boiling it, frying it, even toasting it. And most of them absolutely hated it.

That is how the folklore surrounding salt cod got started. Stories went around that people were using the dried fish as shingles on their barns or saltlicks for cattle or even as snow shoes. "And another story was you'd put it on a slab of poplar," recalls Mcleod. "Put the cod on it and some celery and carrots on it and then you'd cook it. And then throw the cod away and eat the board."

Were the tales true? No one knows for sure, but the Maritimers did not see the humour. "I think they'd be very disappointed that this happened," says Vessey. "I've learned since that they should have sent a recipe with it because there's nothing simpler."

But for Gordon Mcleod and his family, salt cod was no joke. It was a lifesaver. And he is still thankful that the Maritimers sent it. "When I think back to why they sent it, perhaps that's all they had to offer us was some salt cod."

Saskatoon's Western Development Museum still has a piece of salt cod in its collection from the shipments that came to Saskatchewan in the 1930s. It proves how long salt cod can last. It also proves that much of it was never eaten. What the easterners sent with their hearts, westerners just could not stomach.

Just Another Victim

ᕲ

THE SPANISH FLU EPIDEMIC OF 1918–1919 KILLED BETWEEN THIRTY and forty million people worldwide. There has never been a strain of influenza like it. Soldiers returning from the First World War brought the virus over to Canada from Europe. Fifty thousand Canadians died, five thousand in Saskatchewan alone. But one person whose name is on the official list of Saskatchewan casualties didn't die from influenza.

The disease reached Saskatchewan in October 1918. In Saskatoon, the city council banned all public meetings including church services. Schools were closed. The streets were empty. "The town was like a city of the dead," one observer reported.

Highly contagious, the Spanish flu struck with amazing speed, often killing its victims within twenty-four hours. It would begin with weakness, headache, and fever. Patients' skin would become clammy and cold. So much congestion built up that they would eventually drown in their own fluids. The epidemic created such panic and chaos that many people believed the world was coming to an end.

Unlike other viruses, the Spanish flu generally spared children and old people, targeting healthy young adults instead. The president of the University of Saskatchewan, Walter Murray, knew his students were in the high-risk age group. He wasted no time. The university instituted a quarantine. Everyone who wanted to leave was allowed to go. Those who stayed settled in for a long wait. The university, with residences, food services, and its own farms, was uniquely equipped for the quarantine.

The entire campus was sealed off, except for Emmanuel College, which became an emergency treatment centre, staffed by brave volunteers. Most of these volunteers were women. Their names can be found today engraved in the bricks of the old Administration Building. The college was packed from basement to attic with flu victims from Saskatoon and the surrounding area. Many nurses contracted the flu and became patients themselves. Miraculously, of the 120 faculty, staff, and students on campus, only one person died from the flu during the quarantine. Not surprisingly, it was one of the volunteers at Emmanuel College, William Hamilton.

The rest of the university was one of the safest places anywhere. Students lived in residence. Classes continued as usual. Life went on in strange isolation from the disease raging around the world and down the street. The biggest threat to students was boredom.

On the night of Saturday, 9 November 1918, two pharmacy students snuck into the chemistry department. They broke into a lab, drank some methyl alcohol, and then collapsed. When they were found, the students were rushed to City Hospital. One was permanently blinded and the other died from alcohol poisoning.

Walter Murray was reluctant to publicly admit this kind of behaviour could happen at his university, where he had assured parents that their children would be safe during the quarantine. Determined to avoid a scandal, he worked with the coroner who examined the dead

The November 1918 funeral for University of Saskatchewan student William Hamilton, who worked as an orderly in the temporary flu hospital at Emmanuel College. UNIVERSITY OF SASKATCHEWAN ARCHIVES A-5709

student, and they decided together that his death should be attributed to the flu. The flu was claiming so many lives, what was one more? The university succeeded in covering up the incident.

It took years before the truth was discovered. Professor James Sharrard, who had been on the scene that night, wrote it all down in a letter to his wife: "The matter of the pharmacy students was hushed up, the coroner passing him as dying from the flu."

By the spring of 1919, the great flu epidemic was winding down, but it would not completely run its course until 1920. Many Saskatchewan people had been struck down in their prime. Although President Murray had lied about one of those deaths, his quarantine at the university likely saved countless lives. The proof? When the quarantine was lifted and the university reopened in January 1919, there were soon 150 cases of the flu on campus resulting in 6 deaths.

The Accidental Politician

SARAH RAMSLAND MIGHT NEVER HAVE ENDED UP IN POLITICS IF HER husband had not died during the Spanish flu epidemic. Magnus Ramsland, a real estate and insurance agent, had run as a Liberal candidate in the 1917 Saskatchewan provincial election and handily won the Pelly constituency in the east-central part of the province. Within a year, he was struck down by the influenza pandemic that swept the world.

The Saskatchewan government, led by William Martin, thought that the new widow would make a perfect candidate to assume her late husband's seat. Women in the province had secured the vote just two years earlier on 14 February 1916. But those who expected the first elected woman to lead to a new era in Saskatchewan politics would be sadly disappointed. Although suffrage advocates had argued that women had a special contribution to make to political life, Sarah Ramsland would not be the one to do it.

Although Ramsland had come from a political family—her grandfather had sat in the Minnesota legislature—she had shown no interest in any of the Saskatchewan organizations that had been pushing for women's suffrage. She had never been part of the fight for the vote, never joined the women's movement, and never been involved in politics.

Nor was the Martin government interested in putting Sarah Ramsland's name forward as a candidate because she was a woman. Rather, the Liberals were anxious to provide the widow with a decent income, especially since she had three children. Liberal officials also believed that her candidacy would generate a sympathy vote.

Ramsland ran in the 1919 Pelly by-election on the government record. Only one issue dominated the campaign—loyalty. Ramsland was, after all, the loyal widow of a loyal Liberal. Premier Martin made a special visit to the riding, but never once mentioned the party's candidate by name. Women's issues never entered into Liberal campaign strategy.

Sarah Ramsland became the first woman to be elected to the Saskatchewan legislature when she ran as a Liberal in a 1919 by-election to replace her recently deceased husband. SASKATCHEWAN ARCHIVES BOARD R-A7553

Ramsland won the seat by a slightly smaller margin than her husband's two years earlier. But her election generated little interest in the province, and for good reason. Her victory had nothing to do with her gender or women's rights, but simply confirmed public approval of the Liberal record.

Ramsland began her legislative career with high hopes and even higher ideals. After her election, she wrote to her parents, "my own good judgment will be used in every instance . . . my vote can never be bought." Ramsland may have intended to use her position to better her constituency, but she was not much of a leader, and shunned the spotlight. When Premier Martin asked her to second the Speech from the Throne in her first session, she passed on the honour.

During an incident involving future premier Jimmy Gardiner, who was then Minister of Highways, Ramsland showed more spunk. She wanted five dollars to fix a mud hole in her constituency. When Gardiner flatly turned the request down, Ramsland took out her crocheting and threatened to sit there all day until he relented. He did.

If women were expecting an advocate, however, they would have to look elsewhere. Although other members of the legislature tried to make Ramsland feel at home, she felt isolated from her colleagues, likely because of her gender, and rarely spoke. Indeed, her record was entirely unremarkable. For the most part, she behaved like any good backbencher and supported government policy, which allowed her to survive in the male-dominated world of politics.

Ramsland spent six years in the legislature and stood up for women's rights only once. On the last day of the 1925 session, she introduced a resolution calling for an amendment to the divorce law so that men and women could apply on equal grounds. The motion was approved unanimously. It was Ramsland's last act as an MLA; she would lose her seat in the next election. Saskatchewan voters would not send another woman to the legislature for almost twenty years. By then, the member who had first broken the gender barrier had been all but forgotten.

The Blizzard of '47

~

THE YEAR 1947 BLEW INTO SASKATCHEWAN WITH A VENGEANCE. A staggering four feet of snow fell in some parts of southern Saskatchewan—more than double the average. The temperature plummeted to -40°F and stayed there. Then the wind started to howl, hitting speeds of more than seventy miles an hour in several areas. For one long week—from 30 January to 8 February—one of the worst blizzards in Canadian history raged across the prairies. It would have deadly consequences.

The blowing snow created incredibly huge drifts that made travel dangerous, if not impossible. Throughout southern Saskatchewan, rail lines and roads were choked by snow, closing schools, cancelling church services, and postponing social and sporting events. One stretch of track between Weyburn and Talmage, for example, was blocked by a drift that was reported to be eighteen feet high and twenty-four hundred feet long.

Saskatchewan's rural areas were hit the hardest. Many people were completely cut off from the outside world, as telegraph lines were either blown down or buried. With roads closed and trains running behind schedule—if at all—local businesses ran dangerously low on fuel and food.

Farmers responded to the storm as best they could. One dug a tunnel across his yard to his shed, while another cut a hole in the roof of his two-storey barn to get inside to milk the cows. Many lost animals to the bitter cold and drifting snow.

John and Bertha Arnason, seventy and sixty-seven respectively, were no strangers to prairie winters or blizzards. They had lived in the Milestone district since 1906 and were as tough and resilient as any other farm couple.

On 2 February 1947, they were visiting their granddaughter, Helen Schoenfeld, her husband, Arthur, and their two children, who lived on a farm near Ogema. The Arnasons decided they would try to make the most of their visiting time and travel across the fields that day to

Elderly John and Bertha Arnason proved no match for the fierce prairie blizzard. HELEN SCHOENFELD

see their daughter, who lived at Burres, about three miles away from the Schoenfeld farm.

Arthur was reluctant to make the trip, but the Arnasons insisted. They hadn't heard the weather forecast. So Arthur dutifully hitched up the cutter for the cross-country trip. It was cold, but clear and calm, when they set off that afternoon. One mile out, however, they found themselves in the heart of a blinding snowstorm.

The driving snow made it impossible to see anything, even familiar landmarks, and the drifts quickly obliterated the trail and fence lines. Arthur, who knew the land well, was hopelessly lost. Although he did not realize it at the time, they were travelling in a circle.

Arthur hoped that the horses would find their way home, but they soon floundered in the mounting drifts. One fell down and refused to get up. He decided to unhitch the horses from the cutter and set off on foot. He lifted Bertha onto a horse; John walked beside him.

The biting cold penetrated them like stinging needles, quickly freezing their hands, feet and faces. Numbness soon gave way to a deadly drowsiness. Arthur suddenly realized John was no longer at his side. Bertha, meanwhile, had become too weak to sit upright and kept sliding off the back of the horse.

Arthur staggered forward in a frozen daze, dragging Bertha along with him. But he soon realized he would have to leave her if he was going to save his own life. Pushing on alone, he finally saw the light of a farmhouse—ironically, his own—and stumbled home five hours after he had set out.

He told Helen what had happened, then set out again later that night to round up a search party of neighbours. But they were forced to wait out the storm. The frozen bodies of John and Bertha Arnason were found the following day in snowdrifts, just a mile from the Schoenfeld farm. All these years later, Helen vividly remembers the incident and its heartache as if it was only yesterday. After telling Helen what had happened, Arthur never talked about that terrible afternoon again.

Sadly, 2 February would bring more tragedy. Early that morning, St. Patrick's Orphanage in Prince Albert burned down when a fire started in a damp coal pile. Six young girls, aged seven to eleven, perished in the fire, along with a nun. In all, thirty people across western Canada died from the cold in early 1947.

A number of incredible survival stories also emerged from that terrible week of cold. Mrs. H. Thompson gave birth to a baby girl in a cutter while on her way to the Carnduff hospital. John Byneskowski, a veteran of the Normandy invasion during the Second World War, wandered through a storm for twenty-four hours near his home at Stenton before being rescued by his brother. Ollie Forseth, an elderly man who lived alone near Trossachs, endured five days without heat or food when his shack was buried by snow.

The storm finally broke on 9 February. Life began to return to normal as towns dug themselves out of the snow and roads and rail lines were cleared. But the people of southern Saskatchewan knew they would soon face a new challenge from the weather, and began to prepare for the expected spring floods.

Murdered by the RCMP

〜

COAL MINING IS STILL ONE OF THE BIGGEST INDUSTRIES IN THE Estevan-Bienfait area in southeastern Saskatchewan—just as it was in the early twentieth century. But back then, it was a dirty, dangerous job. And when the Depression hit, it got worse. In 1931, the miners never dreamed that they would face their greatest danger above the ground.

Deep-seam coal mining in Saskatchewan was highly seasonal in the early 1900s. Because the lignite coal that was produced had little marketable value except for local consumption, the mines were extremely busy during the winter and then shut down in the summer. The laid-off miners usually found work on local farms.

But in the 1930s, there were few opportunities to work on the land, and mine families became entirely dependent on mining for their day-to-day survival. In addition to a dearth of summer jobs, falling coal prices led to smaller profits for mine owners, who passed these losses on to the miners by drastically cutting wages.

Miners usually worked long hours without breaks. They also had to do extra work, such as pumping water, for which they were not paid. To make matters worse, they worked under extremely hazardous conditions. Safety provisions in the provincial Mines Act were never fully enforced and repairs to mines were rarely carried out. Despite these conditions, the Estevan-Bienfait fields had the highest productivity in Western Canada.

Living conditions for miners and their families were as bad as working conditions in the mines. The sixteen-year-old daughter of a miner, one of nine children, described what it was like waking up in a company house in winter: "When the weather is frosty . . . you cannot walk on the floor because it is all full of snow, right around the room." But miners accepted these conditions in order to keep their families fed, clothed, and sheltered, and perhaps most importantly, to avoid the degrading experience of going on relief. As the Depression deepened, however, miners realized that they needed a union to represent their interests. As things stood, they had no formal grievance procedure, and if they complained they were usually fired.

In early 1931, the miners of southeastern Saskatchewan contacted traditional labour unions for help, but were turned down. They even approached the provincial mines inspector, but were rebuffed. Desperate, they turned to the Workers' Unity League (WUL), an arm of the Communist Party of Canada, which readily agreed to organize the miners into a union. The WUL sent in a representative of the Mine Workers' Union of Canada. An organizational meeting was held on 25 August 1931 in Estevan. Nearly all the miners signed up. They were not Communists, but simply anxious to protect their rights.

Predictably, the employers refused to recognize the new union. The six hundred miners voted to strike on 7 September 1931. Both sides refused to budge, making any kind of settlement impossible.

Over the next few weeks, the employers emphasized the Communist character of the union. Meanwhile, the provincial government bolstered the local RCMP detachment. The striking miners remained peaceful, but refused to negotiate until their union was recognized. When the mine owners and operators started using scab labour, the union organizers decided to hold a sympathy parade in Estevan in order to gain local support.

The striking miners, along with their wives and families, set off for Estevan on 29 September. When their motorcade reached the city, they were confronted with a cordon of mounted police blocking Main Street. The town fire department had also been called out in case hoses were needed to disperse the crowd. Also on hand, if surreptitiously, was Glen Peterson, a lifelong Estevan resident. Thirteen-year-old Peterson skipped school that day and ran downtown to watch. He hid in a metal trash can where he could see everything.

Even when confronted by the police, the miners refused to turn back. When one of them jumped on the fire truck and started hitting it with a crowbar, he was shot dead by a police bullet. A vicious battle ensued. Peterson, from the relative safety of his hiding place, watched as people ran and bullets whizzed by. The miners, wielding clubs and bricks, never had a chance against the Mounties and their revolvers. When it was over, three miners were dead, while eight other miners and several Estevan citizens were wounded. A frightened Peterson was rescued by his frantic father.

The three dead miners were buried together in the Bienfait cemetery. Their headstone reads "Murdered by the RCMP." But Peterson doesn't believe blame should rest completely with the police. "The strikers were putting on a lot of pressure too," he remembers. "It seemed they wouldn't stop."

After the riot, several union organizers and strikers were arrested and convicted of various offences. At the trials, the troubles were blamed on outside agitators and the accused were referred to as radicals and reds. Members of the RCMP, on the other hand, escaped any sort of reprimand. In fact, the police claimed that they didn't draw their weapons until the fighting started. But photographs clearly show the Mounties with their guns drawn much earlier in the event.

In the end, the miners were no further ahead. Their union was not recognized and they were forced to accept an agreement with the mine owners. They went back to the same desperate conditions. It wasn't until 1945 when an American union, the Mine Workers of America, finally organized the coalfields in Saskatchewan, that the miners achieved some control over their working lives.

The Mounties shot and killed three miners during the riot. SASKATCHEWAN *ARCHIVES BOARD R-A8806-1*

Stalked by Fate

IS IT POSSIBLE TO ESCAPE WHAT FATE HAS IN STORE FOR YOU? IN June 1912, a Regina couple found out the answer to that age-old question. They had cheated death in one of the world's most deadly man-made disasters only to come face-to-face with it in one of Canada's worst natural disasters.

Frank and Bertha Blenkhorn married in England in April 1912. They planned to move to Canada right away and begin a new life together. But they became so carried away with their wedding celebration that they missed their passage on the ship that should have taken them to North America. That ship was the *Titanic*.

Supposedly unsinkable, the world's largest and most celebrated ocean liner went down in the North Atlantic after striking an iceberg on its maiden voyage. More than fourteen hundred people lost their lives in the worst peacetime marine disaster in history. The Blenkhorns were spared by their revelry and crossed on another ship.

The cyclone left some residential homes demolished and others—sometimes next door—untouched. SASKATCHEWAN ARCHIVES BOARD R-B3778-10

They must still have been marvelling at their good fortune when they finally arrived in Regina a few weeks later.

Frank began working at the *Regina Standard,* one of the city's three daily newspapers, and later started a real estate business. More than thirty thousand people lived in Regina, and it was the fastest growing city in Canada. The economy was booming; the future looked bright. The Blenkhorns could not possibly have known what was in store for them that summer.

A suffocating heat wave had blanketed the city for several days as the sun rose on Sunday 30 June. The morning was sunny and warm, promising the hottest day yet that summer. It was the Dominion Day holiday weekend and people spent the day going to church and relaxing outside under the clear skies. But by late afternoon, dark, ominous clouds began to develop south of the city. At around 4:30 PM, the Blenkhorns were walking home after spending the afternoon visiting friends. As they crossed Victoria Park, they would have seen the threatening skies, felt the wind pick up, and heard a chilling sound in the distance.

It was no ordinary storm that was brewing. Today, they're called tornadoes: funnel clouds with winds reaching an incredible four hundred kilometres an hour. When they touch down in populated areas, the result can be complete and utter devastation. In the newspapers and history books, the product of the dark clouds that the Blenkhorns saw on the horizon would become known as the Regina Cyclone.

The cyclone struck the city from the south, headed toward Wascana Park, and swept right by the newly constructed Saskatchewan Legislature. It hit the centre of the city with a fury. The Methodist Metropolitan Church was destroyed, and both the YWCA and YMCA buildings were flattened. In the Telephone Exchange building, a massive switchboard crashed through the floor and into the basement, taking the operators with it.

In Victoria Park, the Blenkhorns must have run for their lives. They would not make it. The tornado picked them up and smashed them against the front of the city library. If that did not kill them, the Lorne Street building that collapsed on them surely did.

The tornado carried on, ripping through the Canadian Pacific rail-yards and then striking a residential area. Its path was random.

It destroyed some houses and left others—sometimes right next door—untouched. From start to finish it lasted only five minutes. But its legacy would be felt for years. The Regina Cyclone was one of the strongest tornadoes ever recorded in Canada with wind speeds of between three hundred and four hundred kilometres an hour.

The clean-up took months. Some buildings in downtown Regina, like Knox Presbyterian Church, still bear the scars of the cyclone's onslaught. But the human toll was the most tragic of all. The cyclone killed twenty-eight people, injured two hundred, and left twenty-five hundred homeless. It would have been even worse if the tornado had hit on a busy weekday when the downtown district was full of people.

As for Frank and Bertha Blenkhorn—who defied fate by not boarding the *Titanic*—they died less than three months later in the worst natural disaster Saskatchewan has ever known.

The Debden Miracle

⌒

ALMOST FIFTY THOUSAND CANADIANS WERE KILLED IN THE SECOND World War. Men and women from the tiniest of villages to the biggest of cities gave their lives for their country and for our freedom. But when it all ended in the summer of 1945, one small Saskatchewan town had no reason to mourn and forty-six reasons to celebrate.

When Canada entered the war in September 1939, there was no great wave of enthusiasm. In spite of the Nazi steamroller moving across Europe and rumours of Adolf Hitler's barbarism, Canadians didn't want to get involved in another costly European war. People still remembered the loss and hardship of the First World War. The country had also just come through ten years of depression. But neutrality was out of the question. Prime Minister Mackenzie King announced that while Canada would join the fight against Germany, there would be no conscription; Canada's military contribution to the war effort would depend entirely on voluntary participation.

Canadian men joined up out of a sense of duty and loyalty to the Crown, and the men of Debden, Saskatchewan, were no different. They were farmers, not soldiers, but join up they did.

Debden is a mostly French-speaking, staunchly Catholic community located about one hundred kilometres northwest of Prince Albert. Back in 1939, the parish priest was Monsignor J. E. Joyal. On the eve of war, he made a promise before God and his parishioners. He swore that the parish would build a monument to the Holy Virgin Mary if she brought all the Debden recruits back alive. The Virgin Mary—Christ's mother—is one of the most important figures in Catholic doctrine, infinite in wisdom and in kindness. Of course, the parishioners would have to do their part by praying for their young men's safety each and every day.

Forty-six men from the Debden area answered the call to war. Photos of each of them were placed on the church altar. While their fellow parishioners prayed for them, most of the forty-six made their way into combat. Young and frightened, they bravely went to meet

Monsignor Joyal promised to build a monument to the Virgin Mary if she brought back all of the Debden recruits alive. DEBDEN COMMUNITY CENTRE

their fate. Debden son Leo Beaulac was just twenty-four years old when he arrived in Europe. He still recalls his first night near the front and how he laid awake and cried. His only comfort was a small crucifix his mother had given him.

Canadian soldiers distinguished themselves from Hong Kong to the beaches of Normandy. They played the leading role in the liberation of Holland and are revered by the Dutch to this day. Sailors in the Royal Canadian Navy kept supplies moving on the North Atlantic, running a gauntlet of German U-boats to keep Britain's lifeline open. Canadian fighter pilots squared off with the Luftwaffe, and Royal Canadian Air Force bombing crews dodged anti-aircraft fire over Berlin.

Canada did more than its share to turn the tide against the Axis powers, and the men of Debden were part of it. For six long years, they put their lives on the line for their country. One airman from the community was shot down but parachuted safely to the ground. He was captured by the Germans and spent the rest of the war in a prisoner of war camp. Many others had close calls. Leo Beaulac was shot in the stomach in northwestern Europe. He remembers standing in a doorway during a firefight, feeling like he'd been punched in the side. He took off his belt and discovered two bullet holes. For a while, Beaulac wasn't sure he'd pull through. He wasn't sure the Debden promise would be kept. To this day, he claims he only survived "avec l'aide de Dieu"—with the help of God.

When the war finally ended, the Debden men returned home. Forty-six had left and all forty-six returned safely. One in ten Canadian fighting men lost their lives overseas in the Second World War. At that rate, Debden should have lost at least four or five. Against all odds, they didn't lose one.

People said it was a miracle, that the Holy Virgin had indeed kept her promise by watching over and protecting the men of this small community. Monsignor Joyal kept his promise too. After all the men had returned home, the parish built *Our Lady of Fatima*, a statue that pays tribute to the Holy Virgin, local veterans, and the miracle. It still stands next door to the Catholic church in Debden, and many say that Mary still gives it the power to perform miracles. After all, they have living proof that she performed one before.

Depression Photo

THE FAMILY WAS STRANDED IN EDMONTON'S MARKET SQUARE, barefoot, hungry, and broke: nine people in total, seven of them children, the youngest a three-month-old baby in his mother's arms. A newspaper photographer captured their utter desperation in what would become one of the most enduring photographs of the Great Depression.

Abram and Elizabeth Fehr were German Mennonites from the Nuenlage Colony just north of Saskatoon. They were hard-working, but poor. Abram, a blacksmith, managed to make just enough money to support his growing family. When the Depression hit in 1929, life for the Fehrs became increasingly difficult.

The Depression crippled Saskatchewan. Record-low wheat prices, combined with a prolonged drought, sent shock waves through the entire provincial economy. Businesses and industries were staggered, and the number of unemployed grew with each passing month.

By July 1935, more than two hundred thousand people, almost twenty-five percent of Saskatchewan's population, were on direct relief. Many migrated from the dried-out areas in the south to land along the edge of the northern boreal forest. Others left the province to start new lives elsewhere.

The Fehrs had heard that there was good farming land in Alberta's Peace River country. Desperate for a better life, in 1932 they sold everything they owned, bought an old car, and headed for northern Alberta.

But life in the Peace River country was little better for the Fehrs. Their first crop was hit with frost. The following year, the Peace River flooded. Cornie Fehr remembers the flood as a great adventure. "All the land was flooded. People that lived there moved . . . to their houses in canoes. That's how much water there was all around. As soon as my Dad seen that, he said, 'This is not for us. We're going back.'"

The Fehrs started for home one month after baby Peter was born. For the next eight weeks, they battled mud, breakdowns, and constant hunger. Abram worked at local farms along the way to earn a few pennies to feed his starving family and buy gas for their car. By the time they reached Edmonton on 28 June 1934, Elizabeth was too weak to nurse her baby.

Cornie, ten years old at the time, will never forget what happened. "We didn't have nothing to eat. Dad had no money anymore. And I was elected to go from house to house to beg for food, because I could talk a little English."

Two city police constables found the family and took them to the station, where the Salvation Army gave them food and clothing. "I'd never seen a paper cup in my life," Cornie recounted. "They handed me a cup of milk. I was so thirsty and the milk looked so good, I guess I squashed it a little too hard and the milk went gushing and I started to cry. They told me that was okay, they'd give me some more."

The next day, before the Fehrs left for Saskatoon, a photographer for the *Edmonton Journal* snapped a picture of the family standing in front of their car and trailer. The accompanying article described them as "a pitiful spectacle of depression dereliction." The two city policemen who found the family agreed that the Fehrs' was "the most pitiful case to have ever come to their attention."

Abram and Elizabeth Fehr, with their seven children, became the Depression's poster family. GLENBOW ARCHIVES ND-3-6742

When Abram and his family finally returned to Saskatchewan, he took up blacksmithing again. The years were hard, but they survived without seeking government relief. In 1939, Abram rented two quarter sections of land. "We seeded that," Cornie recalls, "and got a fairly good crop that year. That's when things started looking up, looking better."

Cornie saw the Edmonton photograph for the first time years later in a magazine. Then his granddaughter returned from a trip to Calgary and reported that the picture was prominently displayed in an exhibit in the Glenbow Museum.

Since 1934, the photograph of the Fehr family has come to symbolize the desperate plight of young prairie families during the Great Depression. But the story behind the picture is probably equally important: how thousands of western farmers doggedly survived the bleak 1930s and somehow managed to stay on the land. "I like to look at it and think of what we went through," Cornie remarks, "how we managed and how everybody's doing. How we survived."

The Fighting Bishop

~

ONE OF THE MOST OUTSPOKEN CRITICS OF A MULTICULTURAL
west in the 1920s was George Exton Lloyd. Nicknamed "the fighting
bishop," Lloyd believed in a Canada for the British only and did
everything possible to make it a reality, no matter who he offended.
Born in London, England, in 1861, Lloyd came to Canada as a
twenty-year-old theology student to do Anglican mission work in
Ontario. In 1885, as a member of the Queen's Own Rifles, he partic-
ipated in quelling the North-West Rebellion and was severely
wounded at the Battle of Cut Knife Hill. But his experience did not
dampen his enthusiasm for western Canada and its potential as a
home for prospective British settlers.

Lloyd was ordained as an Anglican priest in Winnipeg in 1885,
and after establishing a boys' school in the Maritimes, returned home
to England with his wife and young family in 1902. He never expected
to set foot in Canada again. But Lloyd was enticed back the following
year, accepting a position as chaplain to the Barr Colony—an attempt
by fellow minister Isaac Barr to create an all-British colony in northern Saskatchewan.

The two thousand Barr colonists experienced a number of problems in getting to Canada and reaching Saskatchewan, all of which
they blamed on Barr. The expedition was poorly organized, lacking
proper food and strong leadership. By the time the colonists reached
Battleford in May 1903, they had lost any remaining faith in their
leader because of his incompetence, and turned to Lloyd to save the
colony. Lloyd took control, to the gratitude of the settlers, who named
their new community Lloydminster in his honour.

Lloyd remained with the colonists for two years before moving to
Prince Albert to become archdeacon and general superintendent of
Anglican missions in the new province of Saskatchewan. Lloyd
believed that Canada, and the West in particular, would realize its
great potential only as a British nation. He was consequently alarmed
by the hundreds of thousands of immigrants from continental Europe

George Lloyd, the so-called saviour of the Barr Colony, was elected bishop for the Saskatchewan diocese in 1922. SASKATCHEWAN ARCHIVES BOARD R-B525

who were taking up the Canadian offer of free homestead land. These "foreigners," as they were called—with their different languages, customs, and religions—represented a distinct threat to his vision of a British West.

Lloyd initially tried to meet the so-called "immigrant challenge" by focusing on the children of the newcomers. He helped bring five hundred British teachers to western Canada between 1916 and 1928 to assimilate school-age children to British principles and traditions. His goal was nothing less than to fashion these immigrant students into good and loyal British subjects.

Lloyd's campaign became more strident after he was elected Anglican bishop for the Saskatchewan diocese in 1922. He was worried that the large number of continental European immigrants coming to western Canada would soon overwhelm the British majority, dragging Canada down and undermining its future.

During the 1920s, Bishop Lloyd became a leading figure in the immigration debate in Saskatchewan. He was not against "foreigners" as long as their numbers were manageable, but he feared that too many were being allowed into the country and that they would never be properly assimilated to the British way of life. The answer, he thought, was strict quotas on non-British immigrants, if not a complete ban.

In 1928, at the height of his anti-immigrant campaign, Lloyd founded the National Association of Canada to lobby the federal government for a drastic reduction in non-British immigration. He pointed out that only nine thousand of the thirty-eight thousand immigrants who came to Canada the previous year were British. He also reportedly sent out an astounding seventy thousand letters to inform people of the issue, and engaged in an extensive speaking tour. He used the strength and influence of the pulpit to spread his message.

Lloyd was colourful and opinionated, but most of all he was fearless in expressing his views. He spoke of Canada becoming a "mongrel" nation and warned of the problems the West would face if the current flood of "dirty, ignorant, garlic-smelling continentals" continued to pour into the country. "The real question at issue," he once declared, "is not whether these people can grow potatoes, but whether you would like your daughter or granddaughter to marry them." This message found a receptive, if not eager, audience among the Anglo-Canadian majority in western Canada. Lloyd was tapping into fears and prejudices about non-British immigrants that already existed below the surface

Lloyd was not alone in trying to preserve Canada as a British stronghold. The Ku Klux Klan was also active in Saskatchewan at the time, and was saying similar things about non-British, non-Protestant immigrants. But Lloyd and the Klan were fighting a losing battle.

In 1931, Lloyd stepped down as bishop and retired to Victoria. He had been unable to hold back the tide of immigrants from Central and Eastern Europe. Many of the so-called foreigners were now Canadian citizens. Their farms and communities were firmly established. Lloyd's nightmare of a multicultural West had taken hold in Saskatchewan.

Lloyd believed that continental European immigrants—with their different languages, customs, and religions—represented a threat to the British West. SASKATCHEWAN ARCHIVES BOARD S-B4591

God's Painter

COUNT BERTHOLD VON IMHOFF WAS BORN IN A CASTLE ON THE Rhine River in 1868. But despite his aristocratic background, he preferred a simpler, more spiritual life—painting for the church. This calling eventually led him to rural Saskatchewan and came at a great personal cost.

Growing up in the German countryside, young Berthold developed a great love of the outdoors and hunting. While still a child he demonstrated a great talent for painting. His profound interest in nature was reflected in his first paintings. With the encouragement of his parents, Berthold studied art and design and quickly developed into a skilled painter. At sixteen, he won top honours for a portrait of Germany's Prince Frederick William. His future career as an artist seemed assured.

But Imhoff was restless. Industrialization—with its noise, pollution, and waste—was ruining his beloved wilderness. After a period of apprenticeship studying the portrayal of religious subjects, he emigrated to the United States. In 1900, he set up his own studio in Reading, Pennsylvania. The count's new business was a resounding success. A devout Catholic, he travelled widely, painting frescos for churches, homes, and businesses.

Despite his success, Imhoff remained dissatisfied. The same industrialization he sought to escape in his native Germany was now changing Pennsylvania. Ever the idealist seeking escape from the modern world, he moved again in 1913 to the quiet isolation of rural Saskatchewan. He bought a half section of land in the St. Marguerite district, near St. Walburg. It was a perfect setting for the count's artistic talents and spiritual needs.

Imhoff's arrival in Saskatchewan coincided with the outbreak of the First World War and, because of his German background, people in the area were initially suspicious of his presence and of his reasons for leaving the United States. But the count quickly won over the local population when he started decorating local church interiors.

In 1937, Imhoff received the title "Knight of St. Gregory the Great" from Pope Pius XI. SASKATCHEWAN ARCHIVES BOARD R-A5648

He built a studio on his farm and painted by the natural light that came through the windows. His forte was Christian art—highly romanticized Biblical themes and figures in a Renaissance style.

The church work was a slow, exacting process. He would first develop miniatures, samples of what he thought would best suit a particular church. He then prepared the huge canvasses in his studio. He would draw out the scene in charcoal, apply a coat of shellac and alcohol, and then paint over this three times—even the smallest detail. His work is noted for its perfect perspective. Once he completed a canvas, he cut it into sections and glued it into position on the walls and ceilings of the church. Imhoff worked only by contract. Throughout his life, he steadfastly refused to sell any of his work privately; he painted for the sheer joy of it.

Imhoff never scrimped. He insisted on using the best paints, the best canvas, the best brushes. Many of his paintings were also lavishly decorated by gold leaf, often painstakingly applied by his son Carl, who served as his assistant.

Imhoff's paintings now decorate dozens of churches of all denominations in west-central Saskatchewan, most notably in the Lloydminster-Battlefords area. Perhaps his most impressive work is to be found in Muenster, where his rich, fulsome style, featuring eighty full-size figures, brings alive the ceilings and sanctuary of St. Peter's Cathedral.

The churches often had little to pay Imhoff for his dazzling work, and with the onset of the Great Depression they sometimes had nothing. Imhoff, however, was known to refuse payment. The work at Muenster, for example, took a full year to complete, but Imhoff considered it his gift to the Church.

By the late 1930s, Imhoff's generosity, combined with his continuing refusal to sell his work, brought his family to the brink of poverty. But the prolific count continued to work for God, giving away paintings, including frescos to his own parish church, now located in Paradise Hill. His kindness and devotion did not go unrecognized. In 1937, Pope Pius XI granted him the title "Knight of St. Gregory the Great" for meritorious service to the church. When Imhoff died two years later at the age of seventy-one, his studio contained over two hundred paintings destined for churches; they are now on display in the St. Walburg museum and in the Imhoff Art Gallery in Lloydminster.

Imhoff was almost penniless at the time of his death. But for thousands of parishioners in rural Saskatchewan, his artistic legacy is priceless. To walk into one of Imhoff's decorated churches is like visiting one of the great galleries or museums of Europe.

Imhoff lavishly decorated the sanctuary and ceilings of St. Peter's Cathedral in Muenster—as a gift to the church. SASKATCHEWAN ARCHIVES BOARD S-B918

Quong Wing

CHINESE CAFÉS HAVE BEEN PART OF THE SASKATCHEWAN LANDSCAPE for over a century. But the people who own and operate them have seen more than their share of discrimination. In 1912, one restaurant owner in Moose Jaw ran into trouble with the law. His crime? Employing two white waitresses.

Right from the start, Chinese people were treated as second-class citizens in Canada. Many came here in the late 1800s as labourers and helped build the country's first national railway. But after the last spike was driven in 1885, the federal government did its best to discourage Chinese immigration. A "head tax" of fifty dollars was levied on each new Chinese immigrant; this tax escalated to five hundred dollars in 1903. In 1923, Canada banned Chinese immigration altogether.

Saskatchewan residents were especially hostile to the Chinese, regarding them as a threat to the moral fibre of white Canada in general and the sanctity of white women in particular. Chinese women were seen as prostitutes, concubines, or slaves. The men were viewed as gamblers, drug addicts, and pimps. Any white woman caught up in their evil influence would surely become a prostitute or opium addict.

In response to mounting public prejudice, the Saskatchewan government passed the Female Labour Act in March 1912. The law forbade white women from working for Chinese employers. It was even a crime for an unaccompanied white woman to visit a Chinese restaurant—except as a customer—or visit any building that was owned or operated by a Chinese person. As one restaurateur would soon discover, the law would be enforced.

Known to locals as Charlie, Quong Wing had run the C.E.R. restaurant in Moose Jaw since 1904. He and the rest of the city's Chinese community were outraged by the Female Labour Act. It was bad enough they had been ghettoized, forced to live in the worst part of town, next to the red-light district. Now this! The community gathered for a meeting and decided to wait for a test case so they could fight the new act in court. They did not have to wait long.

Two months after the law was passed, police raided Quong Wing's restaurant on the corner of Manitoba and Main. He was charged with employing two white waitresses. The trial was held in the Moose Jaw courthouse on May 27.

Wing's lawyer, Nelson R. Craig, argued that his client had been a law-abiding Canadian citizen for seven years, and deserved the same rights as other Canadians. Most Chinese immigrants had not been naturalized, perhaps because many of them expected to return to China one day. The waitresses, Nellie Lane and Mabel Hopham, both testified that Wing was always a "respectable gentleman." They insisted that he treated them well and paid them on time. Craig also pointed out that Quong Wing was also a Christian—a fact that should have held some sway at the time.

The arguments were not enough, though. The judge found Quong Wing guilty, fined him five dollars, and ordered him to fire the two white waitresses.

Wing decided to fight the ruling, first before the Saskatchewan Court of Appeal, then before the Supreme Court of Canada. Quong Wing displayed tremendous courage in carrying on his fight. He must have been motivated by a strong sense of injustice. He also had

Quong Wing had been running the C.E.R. Restaurant in Moose Jaw since 1904. MOOSE JAW ARCHIVES

the support of the Chinese community, which pitched in to help pay for the costs of arguing his case before the highest court in the land.

Quong Wing lost. The greatest legal minds in the country decided that the law was valid: white women needed to be protected from Chinese men and the two races should be kept separate.

Of course, there was no evidence to support the common belief that white women were in any danger. There is no published legal record of the conviction of any Chinese person in Saskatchewan of any sex-related charge at the time. In fact, the Chinese in Saskatchewan had little to do with white society in the early part of the twentieth century. Social contact between the two groups was virtually non-existent.

Despite all the evidence that proved fear to be prejudice, the Female Labour Act was amended in 1925 to allow municipalities to refuse a restaurant or laundry license without giving any reason. The act itself stayed on the books until 1969. Although it wasn't enforced in later years, it remained a symbol of the blatant discrimination Chinese people faced in Saskatchewan.

As for Quong Wing, he lost his legal battle, but at least he started the fight that would one day win Chinese people the same rights as other Canadians.

The Great Soul Rush

HOLY TRINITY CHURCH AT STANLEY MISSION IS NOT ONLY THE OLD-est standing structure in Saskatchewan, it's quite possibly the most beautiful. Built in the 1850s, it stands as a tribute to the Anglican missionaries who brought Christianity to northern Saskatchewan. The church, no longer used for regular Sunday services but open during the summer for baptisms, weddings, funerals, and other special events, has been part of life in Stanley Mission for almost six generations. Almost every resident of the community is Anglican. But everything would have been quite different if Roman Catholic missionaries had won the heated race to claim the souls of the Aboriginal people in that particular region.

In 1845, northern Saskatchewan was home to fur traders and Aboriginal people. The Anglican Church decided there were souls to be saved in this rugged wilderness, and began dispatching its missionaries. The first order of business was to build a church. "One of the local people had a vision of a column of fire going from the point up to the heavens," says Tom Mackenzie, a local historian. "He related that to the missionaries of the time and that's one of the reasons they came to this spot." It would be the spot where they would build not just a church, but a landmark.

At the time, most missions were one-room log cabins, but the church at Stanley Mission was to be a towering structure in the Gothic Revival style. Construction of the massive church was quite a feat considering the location was, and is, accessible only by water.

While the Anglicans were busy building missions in the North, so too were the Roman Catholics. Officials from both denominations felt it was their mission to save the so-called savages from their godless existence and convert them to Christianity. Each believed their best chance of converting Aboriginals to their faith was to get to them first. The churches established a series of competing missions across the North. The great Soul Rush was on.

On the east side of the province, Stanley Mission, Sandy Bay, and

Pelican Narrows became Anglican strongholds. On the west side, the Catholics were dominant. Four future bishops did missionary work at the St-Jean-Baptiste Mission in Île-à-la-Crosse; they offered mass all the way from Green Lake to Fond du Lac.

Many northerners embraced the teachings of the missionaries. Elizabeth Charles lives in Stanley today, and her faith is the foundation of her life. Holy Trinity Church is the symbol of that. "That's where I was baptized and that's where I got married and that's where, I keep telling my children, 'Make sure my coffin is taken to the church and have a service there.' That's what I told them, and keep telling them because it means a lot to me."

The missionaries introduced much more than Christianity. They taught people how to farm and they also built schools, hospitals, and orphanages. At Stanley Mission, only the church remains of what was once a sizeable missionary complex. It has become a landmark and a source of strength. "I thank the Lord that the church is still standing," says Elizabeth Charles. "I always say, 'Thank you Lord for the good night I had and for my health and for the church.' I always look at it when I pray because it gives me strength."

The Great Soul Rush ended in the late 1800s. Who won? It was something of a tie, leaving a legacy that is still evident today. The western half of northern Saskatchewan is predominantly Catholic, while the eastern half is almost exclusively Anglican.

The building of the Church of England mission at Stanley ensured that the east side of northern Saskatchewan would be predominantly Anglican.
SASKATCHEWAN ARCHIVES BOARD S-B590

Naked We Stand

LIKE MANY PRAIRIE COMMUNITIES, YORKTON, SASKATCHEWAN HAS seen its share of protests and marches, from those staged by angry farmers to the upheaval of political rallies. But the town's strangest protest of all happened almost one hundred years ago when the Doukhobors marched into Yorkton—nude!

Seventy-five hundred Doukhobor immigrants arrived in Canada in 1899. The Doukhobors, members of a religious sect that began in Russia, believe that God lives in every person. They believe that priests, churches, even the Bible, are obsolete. Avowed pacifists, they came to Canada as religious refugees, seeking to live in isolated communes and hoping to build new lives free from the persecution they had faced in Russia. When the largest group of immigrants settled in the Yorkton area at the turn of the century, however, it took some time for the locals to get used to their lifestyle and beliefs.

Peter Veregin was the spiritual leader of the Doukhobors. His followers worked extremely hard the first few years, building their villages, clearing their land, and planting their crops. They worked so hard, in fact, that when there weren't enough horses, the women pulled the ploughs to get the crop in the ground. It was customs such as this one that earned the Doukhobors a reputation for being strange and backward. But in many ways, they were ahead of the times.

Ruth Smith still lives in Yorkton. Her father worked at a general store in the years after the Doukhobors arrived. He was impressed with their organization and sense of social equality. "They all ran the village as sort of a business; like a cooperative," Smith recalls. "They shared whatever they made and then they made decisions about how they would spend their money. One of the interesting things about them was that the women were allowed an equal share in the meetings, which was very unusual at that time."

Unfortunately, the Doukhobor's model of socialism came to the province about fifty years too early. Saskatchewan's first socialist government was still decades away. People viewed the Doukhobor lifestyle with suspicion and distrust. Prejudice escalated when a splinter group of Doukhobors began taking their religious beliefs to extremes.

They called themselves the Sons of Freedom. When Veregin suggested that animals should not be exploited, they took his teachings literally and freed their livestock to roam the countryside, burned their leather shoes and went barefoot, and refused to eat meat or dairy products. Such behaviour provoked a reaction. "Probably the same way people would react today," says Ruth Smith. "If people are different, they can't be right. Part of their religion was to try and see a spark of God in every individual and I think the more Christian people try to behave, the harder time they have."

Local people urged the government to do something about their strange and eccentric neighbours. In response, Ottawa decreed that the Doukhobors would have to register their homestead land individually, effectively forcing them out of their communes. The government also asked them to swear allegiance to the Crown— something the Doukhobors associated with military service, which went against their pacifist beliefs.

That's when the protest marches began. And the Sons of Freedom

The Doukhobors held a series of nude marches to protest the federal government's decision that they had to register their homesteads as individuals. SASKATCHEWAN ARCHIVES BOARD R-B6251-1

decided to march nude. Some say it was a religious statement, symbolic of Adam and Eve and their search for the Garden of Eden. Ruth Smith's father believed it wasn't that philosophical. "They didn't really have any way of protesting that would really make people pay attention to them. And they were in danger of losing their land." But going without clothes had its drawbacks. "I know this country is not the country to go march nude in," laughs Smith. "I think after a while they gave up because of mosquitoes."

The naked protestors created quite a stir in Yorkton. Smith thinks her father quite enjoyed the uproar. "I think it was one of the high points of his life. He had never seen nude women before." But he was also saddened by the injustice he saw. "I think Dad felt sorry for them. He didn't feel like they had been quite fairly treated."

The North-West Mounted Police were called in to quell the final Doukhobor protest march in 1908 and it was stopped before it ever really got started.

The protests didn't change anything. The government pushed ahead with its plan to force the Doukhobors to meet the same homestead regulations as other settlers. Angry at what he perceived as betrayal at the hands of Ottawa, Veregin led over five thousand of his followers to British Columbia where they started over. The Doukhobors simply abandoned the homes and farms they had worked so hard to build. A miniature land rush ensued as the Doukhobor property—some four hundred thousand acres—was divided up and resettled. Taking over the Doukhobor property may have been the goal of some locals all along.

Some Doukhobors chose to stay behind. They were forced to give in to the government and take up land as individual homesteaders. Their descendants still live in the area north of Yorkton, and most continue to follow the Doukhobor religion and many of the old customs. And although Peter Veregin moved west, his influence also remains in evidence. The town of Veregin was named after him—a reminder of the utopia that the Doukhobors looked for in Saskatchewan, but never found.

The White Man Governs

❧

THE BODIES OF EIGHT INDIAN WARRIORS LIE BURIED IN A MASS GRAVE on the banks of the North Saskatchewan River near the Battlefords. They all died on the morning of 27 November 1885, but they weren't killed in battle. They died at the hands of an executioner so the Canadian government could send a message.

The 1885 North-West Rebellion was Canada's first and only civil war. Métis leader Louis Riel and his followers were fighting for their rights and culture against a federal government seemingly intent on taking them away.

For the most part, the Indians of the North Saskatchewan country wanted no part of the Métis battle. The chiefs did not support Riel and the uprising. Instead, they chose to remain loyal to the Crown and honour the treaties they had signed. Any Indian participation was sporadic and limited to a few disgruntled bands in the Fort Battleford and Fort Pitt areas.

Prime Minister John A. Macdonald, however, was prepared to use the rebellion as an excuse to crush any remaining vestiges of First

Miserable Man (right foreground) was sentenced to hang along with seven other men. NATIONAL ARCHIVES OF CANADA C17374

Nations autonomy. The federal government wanted to control Indians, to make sure that they stayed quietly on their reserves away from white settlements. It also sought to end a growing treaty rights movement led by the influential chief Big Bear.

In the area that is now west-central Saskatchewan, the Macdonald government identified twenty-eight reserves as disloyal, despite the fact that some of these bands had taken no part in the fighting and had fled their homes in fear of the violence that the uprising caused. The government also secretly adopted a series of measures for the future "management of Indians," including the requirement that Indians could not leave their reserves without a pass and could not sell any of their farm produce without a permit.

The Macdonald government was determined to make an example of any Indians who were brought to trial. There was no shortage of them. Cree chiefs Poundmaker and Big Bear were each sentenced to three years, even though their trials clearly demonstrated that they had acted as peacekeepers during the rebellion. Both chiefs were released early from Stony Mountain Penitentiary, but both died of ill health within a year. Several others received ridiculously long sentences for such offences as stealing a horse or burning a building.

An opportunity for the government to go one step further in its plan to subdue First Nations soon presented itself at Fort Battleford. Eight Indian warriors were charged with murder: Miserable Man, Bad Arrow, Round the Sky, Wandering Spirit, Iron Body, Little Bear, Itka and Man Without Blood. Itka and Man Without Blood were genuinely guilty; they had been settling personal vendettas. Some of the others may well have been innocent but that will never be known because none of them was provided with a lawyer.

In September 1885, with national attention focused on Riel's fate in Regina, all eight were quietly condemned to death. It happened at the hands of one judge, Charles Rouleau. Rouleau had been forced to flee Battleford during the rebellion. When he returned a few weeks later, he found his home, including his collection of legal books, had been destroyed by fire. After that he used his courtroom as a tool for vengeance. Commenting on the fate of the eight "murderers," Rouleau said "It is high time ... Indians should be taught a severe lesson."

The Canadian government arranged to have all eight men executed at once. They also instructed the Indians from the surrounding area to come witness the spectacle. A message was being sent to the First Nations communities in the Battleford area, one that Prime Minister Macdonald put best: "The executions ought to convince the Red Man that the White Man governs."

The executions were fast-tracked. The Governor General signed the death warrants immediately. While the condemned men were shackled and held in cells at Fort Battleford, they would have heard the sounds of the huge gallows being constructed outside. Some accepted their fate. Others protested their innocence. But when Riel was hanged in Regina on 16 November, it became clear they would get no reprieve.

Friday 27 November dawned cold and grey on the gathering crowd at Fort Battleford. One hundred and fifty armed mounted policemen ringed the gallows. Curious townspeople huddled in small groups off to the side, while a large number of Indian families stood in front.

As the condemned climbed the steps, some sang their death songs. Black veils were placed over their heads, followed by ropes. When the priests began their prayers, the signal was given to pull the bolt. The immense gallows strained with the sudden weight. In a few seconds, all eight men were dead. The crowds watched the hangings in silent horror. They quietly moved off as the bodies were cut down and placed in coffins. It was the largest mass execution in Canadian history.

The government got what it wanted. Indians in the area never lifted a hand in defiance again. But the executions marked the low point of First Nations–government relations. More than one hundred years later, the event still haunts the local First Nations.

The Sage of Sintaluta

~

IN 1901, WHEN FARMERS IN THE NORTH-WEST TERRITORIES PRO-
duced the largest wheat crop to date, it seemed that the region was
finally starting to realize its great potential. But neither the Canadian
Pacific Railway nor the elevator companies could handle the record
volume of grain, and half the harvest was lost to spoilage. One man,
Sintaluta-area farmer Edward Alexander Partridge, was determined
never to see such a calamity happen again.

Born on an Ontario farm in 1862, Partridge came west in 1883
and took out a homestead in the Sintaluta area, known locally as "the
Bluffs." He was an indifferent farmer, more given to thinking about
the problems faced by the producer than actually toiling on his land.
He got a chance to put his intellect to work when the large 1901 harvest plugged the grain handling system. Elevators quickly filled up,
and there were not enough boxcars to move the wheat to market.
Farmers were furious.

The breakdown in the grain handling system led directly to a 1902
protest meeting in Indian Head and the formation of the Territorial
Grain Growers Association (TGGA), an organization dedicated to
promoting the collective interests of farmers. Partridge was a key figure in the TGGA from its inception and emerged as a kind of restless
visionary, rarely satisfied by what had been achieved and always thinking of the next step. He argued that the railways, elevator companies,
and grain dealers enjoyed a monopoly and called on farmers to work
together. Only by coming together and speaking with one voice,
Partridge insisted, could farmers begin to exercise some control over
their economic lives. Between 1902 and 1914, Partridge actively pursued a number of ways to end the worst abuses of the grain handling
and marketing system.

After a visit to the Winnipeg Grain Exchange in 1906, Partridge
helped found the Grain Growers' Grain Company: a farmer-owned,
cooperative grain handling company. In 1908, he founded and began
editing the *Grain Growers Guide*, a monthly journal designed to

Partridge argued that the "big interests" of eastern Canada were exploiting the western farmer. SASKATCHEWAN ARCHIVES BOARD R-A 19422

educate the farm community about the need for cooperative action. By the beginning of the First World War, there existed a farmer-controlled cooperative elevator system, which operated both local elevators and Lakehead grain terminals. These initiatives, spearheaded by Partridge, formed the basis of today's United Grain Growers.

Many of Partridge's ideas were quite radical at the time. Farmers had never organized to stand up for themselves before. He took his message to town hall meetings across the West, often neglecting his own operation for weeks, and convinced farmers of the potential benefits of cooperation. Six feet tall and heavy-set, with blue eyes and a handlebar moustache, Partridge was an imposing presence. He quickly earned a popular reputation as the Sage of Sintaluta, an outspoken, driven and at times impractical idealist who refused to compromise. Whatever one thought of Partridge's latest idea or solution, no one could question his commitment or his influence.

By the end of the war, Partridge's thinking had become too radical for most farmers and for other farm leaders. Although he supported the new western-based National Progressive party, he quickly became disillusioned with the party because of its ineffectiveness in Ottawa and its inability to bring about any meaningful long-term political changes. He also began to question whether farmer cooperative organizations went far enough. What was needed instead was fundamental social change—pushing his ideas to the logical conclusion.

Partridge's new vision for western Canada was voiced in his 1926 book, *A War on Poverty*, which called for a radical restructuring of society. Partridge's socialist utopia would be comprised of British Columbia, Alberta, Saskatchewan, Manitoba, and northwestern Ontario and be called COALSAMAO, taking the letters from the names of the provinces. Private property and profit would be abolished in favour of standardization, uniformity, and centralization.

Partridge's new ideas cost him his friends. In fact, the uncompromising zeal that had initially made him such a popular figure now became a liability, and he became increasingly isolated. But he never lost faith in his vision, despite a number of personal tragedies.

He had lost his left foot in a binder accident in 1907 and walked with a heavy limp. The injury caused continual pain and made him irritable. One of his daughters drowned in 1914 while swimming in a slough, and two sons were killed overseas during the First World War. His beloved wife, Mary, died of a heart attack in 1926.

These losses were compounded by deepening debt. Ignoring the operation of his farm to concentrate on his work in the farmers' movement, Partridge sank into poverty and was forced to sell his farm. He moved to Victoria in 1927, where, broken in spirit, he committed suicide in 1931.

Partridge is remembered today as a prairie radical who not only inspired a generation of farmers but whose ideas eventually found a home in the new political movements and parties of the 1930s. Many would argue that prairie farmers today could use another leader like the Sage of Sintaluta.

White Man's Country

~

AT THE BEGINNING OF THE TWENTIETH CENTURY, CANADA SOUGHT to attract farmers to settle the western prairies and cultivate the land. The response was overwhelming. Tens of thousands of immigrants from the United States and Europe answered the call. But some of the settlers who came to Saskatchewan weren't considered the appropriate colour.

In the early 1900s, Canada's population boomed. Thanks to a surging economy, the country grew from 5.3 million people in 1891 to 7.2 million two decades later—a whopping thirty-five per cent increase. From 1901 to 1911, for the first time since the creation of the country, more people came to Canada than left.

Most of the new immigrants headed for the prairies. Newspaper ads and colour brochures in different languages promoted western Canada as a land of great promise and unprecedented opportunity— the "last best West." Prime Minister Wilfrid Laurier claimed the twentieth century would be Canada's century now that the American settlement frontier was closed. All that was needed were people to break the land.

The recruiting campaign caught the attention of Black farmers living in the American West. Most had migrated to what was known as Indian Territory following the Civil War. Slavery was still a fresh memory and discrimination was still rampant. They were intrigued by the Canadian offer of 160 acres of good land for a ten-dollar registration fee.

At first, only a handful of Black families moved north to the Canadian prairies. In Saskatchewan, they settled in the Maidstone district, between North Battleford and Lloydminster, or near Rosetown, southwest of Saskatoon. Joe and Mattie Mayes took land at Eldon, just north of Maidstone, in 1910. The Black community at Maidstone built the Shiloh Baptist Church in 1912 and a school in 1916. Many of the first Black settlers to the province are buried in the Shiloh church cemetery.

Mattie Mayes was one of the original black settlers in Saskatchewan.

SASKATCHEWAN ARCHIVES BOARD R-A 10362

Western Canadians initially took little notice of the Black immigrants, since there were relatively few of them. But when Indian Territory became the state of Oklahoma in 1907 and introduced a number of segregationist measures, Blacks began to move north in greater numbers in order to escape racism. They hoped to find the equality and harmony that eluded them in the United States.

Westerners were alarmed by the influx of Black immigrants, even though the total number of Black immigrants was no more than one thousand. They were already uneasy about the large number of peasant immigrants from continental Europe, with their strange dress, customs, and languages. But they were downright hostile to visible minorities. Westerners regarded the region as a "white man's country" and were not about to share it with Black immigrants, despite their practical farming experience. Something had to be done.

The press spearheaded the campaign against Black immigration. The *Saskatoon Daily Phoenix,* for example, carried a series of articles arguing that the West was no place for Blacks and insisting that the so-called Negro problem was America's problem, not Canada's. Other newspapers perpetuated Black stereotypes, suggesting it was impossible to assimilate the settlers into the Canadian way of life.

Government authorities initiated a number of measures to discourage Black immigration. They pulled all their advertising from newspapers in heavily Black areas of the United States. They conducted rigorous medical exams at the border, sometimes bribing medical authorities to reject Black settlers. They even sent two agents to Oklahoma in 1911 in an effort to bring to an end to any future Black immigration to Canada. The agents were told to talk freely about the hateful reception that Blacks could expect if they moved north, and in this way discourage people from immigrating.

The federal government was worried, though, that these steps would not be enough, and on 12 August 1911, approved an Order in Council banning Black immigration for a period of one year. The document stated that the "Negro race . . . is deemed unsuitable to the climate and requirements of Canada."

The Laurier government never had to use the order, because Black settlers stopped coming to the West. It was formally withdrawn less than two months after it was introduced. It does reveal, however,

The first Black settlers built the Shiloh Baptist Church at Eldon, just north of Maidstone. SASKATCHEWAN ARCHIVES BOARD R-A23399-2

the lengths to which Canada was willing to go to slam the door on Black immigration.

And what of the Black settlers who tried to make Saskatchewan their new home? Despite the frosty reception, they worked their homesteads, built their communities, and raised their families. In the process, even though few remain on the land, they left a legacy of strength and perseverance in the face of adversity and scorn.

One of the greatest success stories is that of Reuben Mayes, grandson of Joe and Mattie Mayes. Raised in North Battleford, Reuben played professional football with the New Orleans Saints and was named National Football League rookie of the year in 1986. The other descendants of the original Black settlers may not be as famous, but they've all made a contribution to Saskatchewan.

It took a long time for the Black settlers to feel at home in the province, to feel like they belonged here. Settling in the West required not only breaking the land, but also dealing with the racism they had come to Canada to escape.

Dickens of the Mounted

$\backsim$

TO A YOUNG MAN IN NINETEENTH-CENTURY ENGLAND, THE NORTH-West Mounted Police represented adventure. To his family, they represented discipline. Such was the situation for Francis Dickens, the fifth child of famous British novelist Charles Dickens. He tried his hand at various occupations, but failed miserably, perhaps because he stuttered and was partially deaf. His father had little use for him and called him "the chicken stalker," implying that he was only capable of chasing chickens.

In 1864, thanks to his family connections, Dickens got a job with the Bengal Mounted Police in India. He returned to London after his father's death in 1871 and spent the next three years drinking away his inheritance.

In October 1874, Frances's family landed him another commission, this time as an inspector with the newly formed North-West

NWMP Inspector Francis Dickens (second from left), the son of British novelist Charles Dickens, had a weakness for alcohol. PUBLIC ARCHIVES OF ALBERTA B1680

57

Mounted Police (NWMP) in Canada. The Canadian government had created the mounted police—a combination soldier-policeman force—to help settle the western frontier. Ottawa wanted to avoid a replica of the wild and woolly American West and looked to the Mounties, in their distinctive red serge, to bring law and order to the prairies.

Dickens spent his first years at police headquarters under close supervision. The commissioner considered him incompetent, lazy, and unfit to lead. Other Mounties believed that the force was no place for him and mockingly nicknamed him Little Charlie. Indeed, men like Dickens gave English recruits a bad reputation. But in 1883 the Mounties took a chance and placed Dickens in charge of Fort Pitt, a quiet trading post on the North Saskatchewan River near the present-day Saskatchewan-Alberta boundary. Two years later, Dickens found himself in the middle of one of the few Indian confrontations of the North-West Rebellion.

On 2 April 1885, Cree warriors killed nine men at nearby Frog Lake in a dispute over the distribution of food. Less than two weeks later, the Cree warriors headed to Pitt to seize the provisions and arms under police guard at the post. A large war party, under the leadership of Chief Wandering Spirit, arrived at the hill overlooking Fort Pitt on 14 April. Although Dickens took initial preparations to defend the post, he soon realized the situation was quite hopeless.

The fort featured a rickety stockade that could easily have been breached. There was also no source of water inside the post walls. Most important of all, the fort lay between the ridge occupied by the Cree and the North Saskatchewan River. The Cree held the upper hand. There was no escape.

Up on the hill, old Chief Big Bear sent an urgent message to Dickens. He promised to hold back Wandering Spirit and his warriors as long as he could if the police surrendered the post. The Mounties would be allowed to leave unharmed while the rest of the fort's occupants became prisoners. Dickens took Big Bear's offer, and early the next evening he and his men boarded a hastily constructed scow and fled down the ice-choked river to Battleford. After they left, Wandering Spirit and his warriors pillaged the post and took hostages. Thankfully, the killings at Frog Lake were not repeated at Fort Pitt. In fact, the prisoners were released several weeks later when the rebellion came to an end.

Dickens was vilified for giving up his post. Some suggested that his retreat had blackened the reputation of the force. But it probably took more courage for him to surrender than to fight. And it was the right decision given the circumstances.

Dickens left the NWMP in the spring of 1886 and went to Ottawa, where he drank heavily. In need of money, he headed to the United States where he hoped to take advantage of his famous name by going on the lecture circuit. What Dickens planned to talk about, though, will never be known. At the age of forty-two, just before he was to give his first talk in Illinois, he dropped dead from an apparent heart attack.

Dickens (right foreground) commanded the NWMP detachment at Fort Pitt during the 1885 North-West Rebellion. HUDSON'S BAY COMPANY ARCHIVES 1987/363-R-34/30 [N13504]

Cowboy Impostor

WILL JAMES WAS ONE OF THE GREATEST AUTHORS AND ARTISTS OF the Wild West. His storybook life took him from a modest homestead in southwestern Saskatchewan all the way to Hollywood.

James started life in 1892 as Ernest Dufault in St. Nazaire, Quebec. As a young boy, Dufault spent all his time sketching on the kitchen floor and devouring dime novels about the American West. He was consumed by a passion to become a cowboy. At fifteen, with only ten dollars in his pocket, he headed for western Canada.

Dufault spent the next four years (1907–1911) roaming the ranch land of southwestern Saskatchewan before slipping across the line to the United States. His exact whereabouts throughout this period are not certain, but it is known that he filed a homestead claim on the Frenchman River near Val Marie, worked as a cowboy on the vast 76 Ranch near Swift Current, started his own ranch in the Cypress Hills near Ravenscrag, and spent time in the Maple Creek jail for his involvement in a bar room shooting. The Dufault homestead is located in the west block of Grasslands National Park, and is a featured stop on the self-guided driving tour of the Frenchman River Valley.

The four years that Dufault spent in southwestern Saskatchewan were fundamental to his development as an artist and writer. The shortgrass prairie, steep coulees, and scruffy badlands of the region fit his childhood vision of the mythical West and would come to dominate his future work as an artist and writer.

It was also in that area of Saskatchewan that Dufault had his first encounter with cattle ranching and the life of the cowboy. He learned about horses, steers, and the range, and was transformed in the process from a greenhorn Quebec teenager into a rugged cowboy and horsebreaker. Dufault's obsession with becoming a cowboy spurred him to bury one past and adopt another. He assumed a new persona, adopting the name William Roderick James and learning to speak English with a western accent to hide his francophone past.

Quebec-born Will James is regarded as one of the greatest writers and artists of the American Wild West. SPECIAL COLLECTIONS, UNIVERSITY OF NEVADA, RENO LIBRARY, 2270/A

With his new identity, James rode into the western United States in 1911 and eventually found considerable fortune as an artist and writer. Claiming to be from Arizona, he worked as a cowboy in Montana, Idaho and Nevada, before getting into trouble again in 1914, this time for cattle rustling. While serving time in Nevada State Prison, he passed the months doing pencil sketches of everyday cowboy life. His illustrations bore a striking resemblance to the Saskatchewan landscape. In fact, people from Val Marie claim that they can see local features in his sketches.

James drifted about the American West before settling in San Francisco in 1919 and enrolling in art classes. The following year, he sold his first set of drawings to *Sunset* magazine. James combined his work as an illustrator with his natural storytelling ability in 1923, when he published his first article, "Bucking Horses and Bucking-Horse Riders" in *Scribner's*, one of America's leading magazines.

The success of the story led to James becoming a regular contributor, and shortly thereafter to publishing his first book, *Cowboys North and South* (1924). Over the next eighteen years, James wrote and illustrated twenty-three books, including the hugely successful *Smoky* (1926), and his fictionalized autobiography, *Lone Cowboy* (1930). His books were translated into several languages, and many had several printings.

What made these books so appealing was the way in which James so effectively captured the idealized, romantic West of yesterday, where the quintessential American cowboy was a solitary figure and his best friend was his horse. He did so through his colourful, western vernacular style, his intimate knowledge of cowboy life, and his realistic sketches, especially of horses. James took great pains to emphasize the authenticity of his stories. "I am a cowboy," he stated in the preface of his first book, "and what's put down in these pages is not material that I've hunted up, it's what I've lived, seen, and went thru before I ever had any ideas that my writing and sketches would ever appear before the public."

In 1926, James bought a large ranch in southern Montana, named the Rocking R, and used his publishing income to start a cattle operation. He also began spending time in Hollywood, where he worked as a stunt rider and his books were made into movies.

By the early 1930s, James was one of the most famous cowboys in America. But his past haunted him. He was afraid that his true identity would surface and he would be branded an impostor. In 1934, he secretly returned to Canada in an attempt to destroy anything that would link him to Ernest Dufault.

James's fear of exposure soon overwhelmed him, and he began drinking heavily. He lost his wife, his ranch, and then his health. He died in Hollywood in 1942. He was just fifty years old.

It's been said that the Wild West could make or break a man. For Will James, it did both. It made a character who was larger than life, and broke a man who couldn't live with his secret past.

This is the story of a cowboy and a cowhorse — born on the same day — They growed up together to where they was big enough — Big Enough for most anything —

WILL JAMES '31

Will James sketch, Big-Enough.
NEW YORK: CHARLES SCRIBNER'S SONS, 1931

The Saskatoon Lily

⌒

IN THE FALL OF 1925, SEVENTEEN-YEAR-OLD ETHEL CATHERWOOD enrolled in her last year of high school at Bedford Road Collegiate in Saskatoon. She was beautiful, talented, and athletic, and would go on to Olympic glory. But at the height of her fame, Ethel would turn her back on Canada and walk away from sport.

Ethel Hannah Catherwood was born in North Dakota in April 1908, but was raised on her family's homestead near Scott, Saskatchewan, about one hundred miles west of Saskatoon. One of nine children, she was a natural athlete; she played baseball, basketball, and even hockey, which was unusual for women at the time. Encouraged by her father, Ethel began to high jump in her family's backyard before she was ten. She was soon jumping heights that rivalled those cleared by any other woman in the world at the time.

In 1925, the Catherwood family moved to the Caswell Hill district of Saskatoon. Ethel competed in the city track-and-field championships the following summer and easily won the high jump event with a jump of 5 feet, the Canadian women's record at the time. Her victory was reported without fanfare in the local newspaper, but when Joe Griffiths, director of athletics at the University of Saskatchewan, noticed the height he knew that Ethel was something special. Griffiths visited the Catherwood family at home and watched in amazement as Ethel cleared the high-jump bar in the cramped backyard with ease.

Ethel immediately began training with Griffiths, and within weeks was regularly jumping 5 feet, 2 inches. Griffiths tried to teach Ethel how to do the western roll, but she remained more comfortable with the traditional scissors kick. Later that fall, at the 1926 Saskatchewan provincial championships in Regina, she set a world record with a height of 5 feet, 2$\frac{7}{16}$ inches.

The following summer, Ethel travelled to Toronto under the sponsorship of the Saskatoon Elks Club and jumped before fifteen thousand spectators at the Canadian National Exhibition. Her western roots, together with her exceptional beauty, earned her the nickname "the Saskatoon Lily." For a nineteen-year-old prairie girl, it must have seemed like a dream.

In February 1928, the Canadian Olympic Committee invited Ethel to Toronto to train for the coming games in Amsterdam. It would be the first time women were allowed to compete officially, and Ethel would be ready. At the Canadian Olympic qualifying meet in Halifax on 2 July 1928, she set a new world record with a height of 5 feet, 3 inches. It would remain the Canadian record for the next quarter-century.

Ethel travelled to the ninth Olympic Games as a member of the six-woman Canadian track team. Known as "the matchless six," Florence Bell, Ethel Catherwood, Myrtle Cook, Fannie Rosenfeld, Ethel Smith, and Jean Thompson would win the team championship—an ironic outcome, since Canada was one of the countries initially opposed to female participation in the games.

Ethel competed on Saturday, 5 August, the last day of the track events. It was the most anticipated showdown of the games. Less than three weeks after Ethel's record-breaking jump in Halifax, Carolina Grisof of the Dutch team had beaten her record. The pair was now expected to compete for the gold.

Ethel (third from left) and other members of Canada's 1928 Olympic team.

Ethel's western roots, together with her exceptional beauty, earned her the nickname "the Saskatoon Lily." SASKATOON PUBLIC LIBRARY, LOCAL HISTORY ROOM LH665

The cold windy weather quickly whittled the competition down to three women: Catherwood, Grisof, and an American jumper. Ethel cleared the bar at 5 feet, 2 9/16 inches. When the other two failed on their third attempts at that height, the spectators rushed onto the field and lifted Ethel to their shoulders.

Ethel became an overnight sensation. A *New York Times* reporter dubbed her the prettiest girl at the games, and she returned to civic receptions in Montreal, Toronto, and Winnipeg. There were parties and parades wherever she went. In Saskatoon, the mayor declared 26

September 1928 a civic holiday, Ethel Catherwood Day, and presented Ethel with three thousand dollars to help fund her education. Hollywood even came calling, and there was talk of a movie career.

Then her world began to fall apart.

A talented musician, Ethel returned to Toronto in October 1928 to study music at the Royal Conservatory. But less than a year later, she abruptly withdrew from the program—without explanation—to enroll in a secretarial course.

Ethel continued to train, but nagging injuries prevented her from equalling her past achievements. Her high-jumping career came to a sudden end in 1931 when she placed third at the Canadian track-and-field championships. It was the first time she had lost the event, and in doing so she failed to qualify for the 1932 Olympics.

Things would get worse. In December 1931, the press discovered that Ethel had secretly married a Toronto bank clerk in 1929, may have become pregnant, and was now seeking a divorce. Such behaviour was considered scandalous at the time, and rumours of promiscuity began to wilt her image as the Saskatoon Lily.

It appears that instant fame and success had overwhelmed her, and she could not handle all the pressure and the media attention. Nor was she prepared for failure.

Bitter and disillusioned, Ethel turned her back on Canada, her family and her sport, and moved to the United States. She remarried in 1932, this time to the coach of the United States rowing team, who she met in Amsterdam. She lived in Detroit for a brief period before relocating to San Francisco. In 1960, she divorced again and began working as a stenographer.

On the fiftieth anniversary of her Olympic victory, Canadian sports reporters went looking for Ethel and found her living in seclusion in Palo Alto, California. When contacted by telephone, she told reporters that she had sold all her medals and trophies, had no use for sports or Canada, and simply wanted to be left alone.

But Saskatoon could not forget her. In 1986, Ethel was inducted *in absentia* into the Saskatoon Sport Hall of Fame as one of the greatest female athletes in Saskatchewan history. One year later, Ethel died in obscurity. To this day, she remains the only Canadian woman to win a gold medal in an individual track-and-field event at the Olympics.

The Welwyn Massacre

By the late 1800s, the industrial revolution had created squalid conditions in many English cities. A British philanthropist named Thomas Barnardo conceived the idea to send the orphans and street children from these cities to Canada, where they could begin new lives as farmhands and labourers. They became known as Home Children, and eight thousand of them were sent over between the years 1882 and 1902. Most of the Home Children were placed on Canadian farms. Some were treated well and accepted as part of their host families. Others were abused and worked like slaves. One of the children sent from England to Canada was an orphan named John Morrison. His story is one of injustice, forbidden love, and murder.

Dave Brindle is an author and broadcaster who has researched the life of John Morrison. He says little is known of Morrison's life in Canada except that he grew up and worked his way across the country. In 1895, at the age of 22, Morrison ended up on a homestead near Welwyn, Saskatchewan—near the Manitoba border—working for Alex McArthur. McArthur was both postmaster for Welwyn and a farmer supporting his wife and children.

"I think McArthur was a mean man," says Brindle, who grew up near Welwyn. "Mean to his family and inconsiderate to his wife. And I think his business, which was cattle, was more important to him than his family."

Morrison spent five years working on McArthur's farm. That may have been because of McArthur's fifteen-year-old daughter Maggie, a beautiful and vivacious girl. The hired hand became infatuated with the girl, and that infatuation would develop into an obsession. Brindle believes that Morrison's interest in Maggie would not have gone over well with Alex McArthur. In fact, he believes there was likely a confrontation. A hired hand in his twenties courting the young daughter of a community leader would have been unthinkable. But what John Morrison did in revenge was even more unthinkable.

Mr. and Mrs. Alex McArthur died at the hands of an axe-wielding John Morrison. MOOSOMIN WORLD, 14 JUNE 1900

On 8 June 1900, John Morrison returned late to the McArthur farmhouse after an evening of playing soccer and drinking with other hired hands at a neighbouring farm. He grabbed his axe from the barn, entered the house, and headed for McArthur's bedroom.

First he attacked Alex in his bed. The father of seven was found with deep axe wounds in his head. According to Brindle, Morrison intended to take only one victim that night. "He didn't expect Mrs. McArthur—who was lying with one eye open because she had a two-week old baby—to wake up and look at him and say, 'Oh!' He takes the axe to Mrs. McArthur and then he has the bizarre thought, 'Mrs. McArthur is dead. Perhaps she would like to have her children with her.'"

Morrison continued his bloody work: four-year-old Russell, eleven-year-old Dempsey and eight-year-old Charlie, the same children he had been playing with just hours earlier, all lay dead. And the axe continued to rise and fall. Morrison attacked three more McArthur children, including the baby, but these children survived. Only Maggie, the object of Morrison's desire, was spared.

Covered in the family's blood after the killing spree, Morrison sat on the edge of Maggie's bed as she cowered beneath the covers. No one is sure what he said or did. Then he quietly left the house and went to the barn where he kept a shotgun. He put it to his chest and pulled the trigger. After hearing the blast, Maggie ran barefoot to a neighbouring farmhouse for help.

When a group of men arrived at the McArthur house, they discovered that John Morrison was not dead. Somehow the shotgun had slipped, leaving Morrison with a gaping wound in his side. "They immediately wanted to lynch Morrison," says Dave Brindle. "But cooler heads prevailed." Morrison was taken to jail. A few days later, the victims of the massacre were buried. Their gravestone still sits in the Moosomin cemetery.

John Morrison recovered from his wound and admitted to the killings. He was hanged for his crimes seven months later in Regina.

"I think probably he had a borderline personality disorder," explains Brindle. "I think he had lived his whole life with rejection and abandonment. And I think he found a situation for himself with the McArthurs that gave him a home. That gave him what he perceived as a family for the first time in his life. And when that shattered and proved to be false, he snapped."

Relatives took in the surviving McArthur children. Maggie—obviously traumatized by what had happened—died of unknown causes just twelve years later. As for the Home Children, thousands of them built new lives for themselves and became good citizens, no matter how they were treated upon their arrival in Canada. Only one, John Morrison, made a name for himself as a madman.

Fly Boys

FOR MORE THAN SIXTY YEARS, THE CANADIAN FORCES BASE IN MOOSE Jaw has served as an international flight training school. Pilots and crews still come to learn the intricacies of military flying. The tradition began during the Second World War, when thousands of dashing young airmen—mostly from Great Britain—were shipped to Saskatchewan for training. That made the Moose Jaw girls very happy, and the Moose Jaw boys very jealous.

The British Commonwealth Air Training Plan (BCATP) was one of Canada's major military contributions to the Allied cause. Over 130,000 international pilots and ground crew were trained here. Saskatchewan's flat terrain and sunny skies made it a perfect home for the BCATP, and 21 flight schools were established in the province. Moose Jaw's was one of the biggest. The training plan was the biggest reason most Saskatchewan men signed-up for the air force instead of the army.

Men from places like Australia, New Zealand, India, and other Commonwealth countries began arriving in Moose Jaw in 1940. Most of the international trainees, however, were from Britain. The presence of all these new men caused quite a stir in the community. Romances between Moose Jaw girls and British airmen became quite common.

Marion Tolley was seventeen years old at the time. Her sister began dating a Scottish pilot. Marion herself fell for a young English airman. "I looked across the room," she recalls. "And the blondest man—blondest person maybe—that I'd ever seen, with the bluest eyes and fairest skin and a charming smile, I just fell in love at first sight."

By 1944, most of the local men were overseas fighting for king and country. But a handful—those too young to serve or unfit or unwilling to fight—remained in Moose Jaw. They weren't too keen on the idea of their women being swept away by the fancy-talking fly boys. Tensions rose. A rivalry began to simmer that boiled over at a Saturday

Marion eloped with her British sweetheart, George Tolley (front right), and went to live in England for a few years. MARION TOLLEY

night dance in September 1944, when a fight started between a member of England's Royal Air Force (RAF) and a local boy from Moose Jaw. The fight escalated into a brawl in the alley outside, and local police were called in to break it up.

But the worst was yet to come.

Skirmishes were reported over the next few days. Insults flew, with RAF members questioning the patriotism and courage of the local men for not being part of the war effort—did they have flat feet or cold feet? In turn, the locals heckled the airmen, calling them "yellow-bellied, English bastards."

The following Tuesday, four British airmen were ambushed and knocked unconscious in a downtown park. Word of the attack reached the Temple Gardens dance hall, where 350 RAF members were gathered. They poured into the streets. The showdown was on. Fights broke out all over town. It turned into a full-scale riot.

When it was all over, five people had been arrested. Dozens more were bloodied and bruised. The RCMP investigation blamed the British airmen. Not surprisingly, military police found the unruly Moose Jaw boys at fault.

Two months later, with the war beginning to wind down, the Moose Jaw airbase was closed, although it reopened in 1952. But many of the relationships that had formed continued on. Marion Tolley eloped with her British sweetheart George Tolley and went to live in England for a few years. The story was the same for dozens of other Moose Jaw girls. Many of them, including Marion, eventually returned to the Canadian prairies with their British husbands.

Strangely enough, Moose Jaw's flight school was the only training centre in the country where relations between trainees and locals turned ugly. While the Canadians and British were fighting side-by-side overseas, they were bitter enemies in Moose Jaw, fighting for the attention of local girls.

The Reluctant Giant

~

IN THE EARLY 1900s, A YOUNG MAN NAMED EDOUARD BEAUPRÉ
became a star in the Barnum and Bailey Circus and put his hometown of Willow Bunch, Saskatchewan, on the map. Beaupré, who
grew to over eight feet tall, is still the main attraction at the Willow
Bunch museum. You can see his baptismal certificate, lie down in his
nine-foot bed, and, most importantly, visit his grave. But it was not
always like that. It took almost a century for his remains to come
home. Beaupré was exploited in death just as he had been in life.

Born in 1881 in the French-speaking, Métis community of Willow
Bunch, Edouard was the first of twenty children in his family. His
height and weight started out normal. But a tumour in his pituitary
gland began to affect him when he turned three, and he just kept
growing. By the time he was nine years old, he was already over six
feet tall. Beaupré would eventually top eight feet, three inches, and
weigh four hundred pounds.

Many of Beaupré's descendants still live in the Willow Bunch area.
His story has become legendary. Ovila L'esperance is Beaupré's
nephew and knows his uncle's story well. He says the friendly giant
was extremely shy and was never comfortable with the attention he
generated. Beaupré left school when he was just fifteen to work on
ranches in the area. All he really wanted was to become a cowboy, but
his size got in the way.

"He had a saddle horse, a smaller horse," says L'esperance. "It
weighed around eight hundred pounds, so Edouard's feet would drag
on the ground. And there wasn't that many horses bigger than that at
the time. But he would do tricks. He would make his horse walk from
under him and make the kids laugh."

The tricks he performed with his horse provided Beaupré with his
first taste of performing. He soon realized that would be the only way
he could help support his family. He went from riding horses to lift-
ing them as part of his act.

Beaupré decided to go on tour across Canada and the northern

Beaupré was a star in the Barnum and Bailey Circus, but he hated being on display. SASKATCHEWAN ARCHIVES BOARD R-A3465

United States when he was just seventeen years old. He became the star attraction in the freak show with Barnum and Bailey's travelling circus. His show business name became "The Willow Bunch Giant."

But Beaupré's fame did not garner him fortune. Although intelligent (he was fluent in four languages), Beaupré was uneducated and gullible. As a result, unscrupulous agents and promoters often cheated him. Still, he faithfully sent home what money he could.

Edouard hated being on display, loathed being presented as a freak. He quit the circus after four years and came home for a while. But show business was the only way he could earn a living. He went back out on the road when he was twenty-two years old. He wouldn't live to see twenty-four.

Like many of history's largest people, Edouard died young. The official cause of death was tuberculosis. He passed away while performing at the St. Louis World's Fair in 1904. His family was told he had been buried there. It was a lie. Ovila L'esperance says people still wanted to make money off his famous uncle. "They had a scheme. They didn't want the body to go."

Beaupré's agent at the time had Edouard's body mummified and put on display. Even in death, Beaupré continued to be treated as a freak. The body was eventually sold and shipped to Montreal, where people continued to pay to see it. Eventually, the University of Montreal claimed the corpse after it had been abandoned in a warehouse. But there would be no rest for Edouard Beaupré. University officials kept Beaupré's remains on display, in spite of their deteriorating condition, until 1975, when Ovila L'esperance decided to do something about it.

"To leave a person like that—exposed to the public—I didn't think it was right," says L'esperance. "So I went with my sister and she said, 'Yeah, we should try to do something about that.'" The family launched a legal battle to bring their famous relative home. "It took me about twenty years to do something. They didn't want to part with him." Finally, in 1990, Edouard Beaupré's remains were cremated and returned to Saskatchewan. The Willow Bunch Giant had finally come home.

Scott's Secret

WALTER SCOTT WAS NOT ONLY SASKATCHEWAN'S FIRST PREMIER, BUT also one of the best. Scott, however, had a dark secret that tormented him until the day he died.

Walter Scott was born in 1867 near Strathroy, Ontario, the illegitimate son of a farmer. He left for western Canada when he was just eighteen years old. He settled in Regina and began working in the newspaper and printing business. He was very successful, and eventually bought the *Moose Jaw Times* and the *Regina Leader*. Scott's business savvy made him a wealthy man, which allowed him to try his hand at politics. He became Saskatchewan's first premier in September 1905.

Those first few years in office were heady days. Saskatchewan was the fastest-growing province in Canada. Scott's government selected Regina as the capital and founded the University of Saskatchewan in Saskatoon as a consolation prize. Always possessed by a spirit of fairness, he built the provincial jail in Prince Albert and the insane asylum in Battleford. Scott's crowning achievement was building the province's new legislature. The building took four years and $1.8 million to construct.

Scott was popular with the press and with the people, because publicly he was extremely optimistic and confident that Saskatchewan was going to be the biggest and best province in Canada. Privately though, it was a different story. By the time the new legislature was opened in 1912, the man behind it was not there to officiate. Premier Walter Scott was away, being treated for mental illness.

Scott suffered from manic depression. The premier would experience periods of great activity and happiness, particularly in the summer. He'd be busy leading political rallies, holding meetings and writing letters. But come November, he would fall into a deep depression. He may have suffered from an extreme form of what's known today as seasonal affective disorder (SAD).

Beginning in 1907, Walter Scott began missing entire legislative sessions. He would flee the province for five or six months every year to escape winter and seek treatment for his depression. He travelled to the United States and Europe. He tried horseback riding, golf, ocean voyages, almost anything to find a cure. But his nervousness and agitation only got worse. Scott was desperate. He spent a lot of

During his eleven years as premier, Walter Scott was in Saskatchewan for only half his tenure. SASKATCHEWAN ARCHIVES BOARD R-A245

time and a lot of money looking for answers. He called his depression "the black cloud over his shoulder" or "impending doom." Scott dreaded the end of every summer, dreaded the onslaught of another bout of depression.

The premier was a prolific letter-writer. He left behind dozens of personal letters in which he wrote frankly about his mental illness. On 5 May 1913, for example, he wrote, "I had a pretty bad time during a long course of months. From November, 1911, during most of a year, I was suffering very decidedly from what is commonly called nervous prostration, i.e. exhaustion of nervous energy. I was depressed and under a sense of impending calamity all the time." Many of his letters overflowed with newfound hope. On 13 May of the same year he wrote, "I am now as hard as nails and the awful depression which I suffered continuously during eight or ten months does not trouble me at all anymore. In fact, I feel better than I have felt for many years; appetite good, keen for work, cheerful all the time." His sense of hope, however, never lasted long.

As his illness worsened, Scott began leaving Regina more and more often. In fact, during his eleven years as premier, he was in Saskatchewan for only five and a half years. Scott's deputy premier, James Calder, and the rest of his cabinet ran the government. They covered up Scott's illness, and most Saskatchewan residents never had a clue their leader was manic-depressive.

Despite his malaise, Scott won three consecutive provincial elections with a larger majority each time. But finally, in 1916, it all fell apart. Scott lost it in the legislature. He began hurling insults at one of his political opponents, referring to him as a "moral leper." Behaviour like that was unheard of during legislative sessions, and even Scott's own party realized he had gone too far. He had crossed the line of civil debate. The premier was forced to resign. With his political career in tatters, his depression became worse.

Walter Scott eventually returned to his home province of Ontario. The man who gave Saskatchewan women the right to vote, founded the provincial university, and built the legislature died alone and forgotten in a mental asylum in 1938.

Skates

~

THERE ISN'T MUCH LEFT OF FLORAL, SASKATCHEWAN, THESE DAYS. but the few people who do live in the area still like to claim Gordie Howe as their own. Howe was born there in 1928, but his family moved to Saskatoon when he was just nine days old. There is a very good reason for Floral residents to claim Howe, of course: he is still considered the greatest athlete to ever come out of Saskatchewan.

Growing up during the Depression meant there was not much to do for Howe except play sports with his neighbourhood pals. His two favourite games were baseball and hockey. Nobody could afford much in the way of equipment at that time, but Howe and his friends would use home-made hockey sticks or salvage broken ones from the local rink. Skates were a luxury few could afford. All his early hockey was played on the streets in shoes or boots, but Howe never let that slow him down. He would spend hours shooting tennis balls against the side of the family house. When he finally got his hands on a real puck the house took an even worse beating. And when he got his feet into skates, his talent exploded.

Howe would become known as "Mr. Hockey," and would dominate professional hockey for decades, winning four Stanley Cup championships, setting countless records and playing well into his fifties. None of this would have happened if fate hadn't knocked on his door, or if his mother hadn't answered.

During the Great Depression, Katherine and Albert Howe were struggling, trying to raise eight children. One night in the winter of 1933 there was a knock at the door. When Katherine answered the door, there was a woman standing on the front step with a sack. Desperate for food for her children, she begged Mrs. Howe to buy the contents of the bag from her. Katherine, concerned and caring as always, scrounged around the house and came up with a couple of dollars and some food stamps. The woman took the money and disappeared into the night.

After the woman left, the Howe family opened up the sack and dumped the contents on the floor. Out fell an old pair of large hockey skates. Gordie, then just six years old, fought with his sister Edna over who would get the skates. They each grabbed one. For several days, they each attempted to negotiate the ice with just one skate. Eventually, Edna gave up and Gordie claimed the other skate. He stuffed the toes with paper, laced them up, and went to the rink to skate for the very first time. In a way, he never really came back from the rink.

Howe was a natural athlete. Tall for his age and broad-shouldered, he was soon far ahead of his teammates and opponents. His skills with a hockey stick were unmatched, but the characteristic that most defined him was his fiery intensity. Howe could be downright intimidating. That on-ice nature was in stark contrast to the shy, quiet kid most people knew.

Howe played his junior hockey with the Saskatoon Lions. At the age of fifteen, he went to his first professional training camp. When he hit the National Hockey League in 1946, no one could have predicted how he'd dominate the game for the next three decades. Howe made the top ten in scoring for twenty-one consecutive seasons. He

Howe (back row, centre) was a natural athlete—he was soon head and shoulders above his teammates and opponents. GLADYS LYALL

set league records for goals and assists, and for penalty minutes. He led the Detroit Red Wings to four Stanley Cup victories. Perhaps most impressive was his longevity. Howe played professional hockey until he was fifty-one years old. He had his most productive NHL season, with forty-four goals and fifty-nine assists, when he was forty-one. He even got to play on the same team with his sons Mark and Marty. Howe accomplished all of this with a unique combination of finesse and brute strength. Besides the nickname "Mr. Hockey," Howe has also been called "Elbows" and "Power."

Other nicknames have also surfaced. On Gordie Howe's official Web site, he is referred to as "Mr. Destiny." That could not be any closer to the truth. If Katherine Howe had not unknowingly purchased that pair of skates, it would have been years before the Howe family could have afforded to buy skates for him, years before he got the chance to do what he did better than anybody else.

Although they tried, the Howe family never found out who the woman was or what became of her. They certainly do not know why she chose their door to knock on with an old pair of skates to sell. But they know they owe her a debt of gratitude, and so do the millions of hockey fans who cheered Gordie Howe throughout his extraordinary career.

Sukanen's Dream

～

TOM SUKANEN HAD A DREAM. HE PLANNED TO BUILD A SHIP IN THE middle of the Canadian prairies, launch it into the South Saskatchewan River and sail it all the way back home to his native Finland. Sukanen was an accomplished shipbuilder who emigrated from Finland to Minnesota in 1898. After struggling to grow crops on poor land for fifteen years, he decided to start over again in Canada. Leaving his wife and children behind, he homesteaded near Macrorie on the South Saskatchewan. Short and notoriously strong, Sukanen was incredibly inventive, knitting his own work clothes out of binder twine and building his own threshing machine, among other devices. He gained a reputation as something of an oddball.

He returned home on foot to collect his family in Minnesota in 1919, five years after he had left, only to discover that his wife had died in the Spanish flu epidemic of 1918 and his four children had been adopted out. Distraught, Sukanen returned to his farm in Saskatchewan. As the years passed, his behaviour became more and more erratic. In 1929, he became homesick and decided to return to Finland. So he launched a rowboat on the South Saskatchewan River, somewhere around Outlook, and incredibly, rowed all the way to Hudson Bay, a trip of over six hundred miles. There, he caught a freighter to take him across the ocean. He was a man to whom time and distance seemed to mean very little.

Sukanen returned to Canada the following spring, but later that same year a shipment of supplies arrived at Macrorie that proved he wasn't there to stay. For the next decade, he set to work building a thirty-three-foot, ocean-going steamship, complete with wheelhouse and cabins. Tom Sukanen was going home again. And this time his plan was to sail all the way from Macrorie to Finland. Some of his neighbours tried to help him. Others thought he was crazy.

The ship became an obsession. Sukanen ignored his farm and worked all hours of the day and night. He seldom stopped to eat and would not talk to anybody. By 1941, the boiler and engine were

Tom Sukanen was determined to return home to Finland by building a boat that would take him from the middle of Saskatchewan to Hudson Bay and then across the North Atlantic. MOOSE JAW PIONEER VILLAGE

finished. By 1943, Sukanen was dragging the ship towards the river, section by section. But one night, only four miles from the river, the ship was vandalized and Sukanen—already suffering from nervous exhaustion—broke down.

Tom Sukanen's neighbours had him committed to the Battleford asylum. He died there later the same year without ever realizing his dream of sailing from the prairies to his homeland halfway around the world.

Decades later, Sukanen's ship was recovered and restored by a group of volunteers. The people who painstakingly pieced it together maintain there is no reason in the world that Sukanen's ship could not have made the voyage for which it was intended. It is still on display at a museum just outside of Moose Jaw.

Canada's Sweetheart

~

D<small>URING THE SECOND WORLD WAR, CANADIAN SOLDIERS WERE OVER</small>-seas fighting for their lives. They hung on to any little reminder of home, anything that could give them hope. For many, it was a pin-up of an unknown beauty from Saskatoon.

Mollie Hough still vividly remembers her experiences during the war. She married her husband, Lou, in 1943. It was a chaotic time for both of them. He was with the Royal Canadian Navy, sailing the North Atlantic supply routes and fending off German U-boats. Mollie was home in Saskatoon, eager to contribute to the war effort. "One day, I said 'Enough is enough!'" she recalls. "The men aren't getting this war over with. I'm going to see about joining up."

Mollie signed up with the navy and was sent to Galt, Ontario, for training. One fateful day in June—in about as long as it takes to snap a picture—she would go from being just another recruit to being an international sex symbol.

"The officers asked some of us if we would like to go to a swimming pool and it was very hot and very humid. The only rotten thing about it was that they would not let us get in the pool until they had taken some pictures. So when I'm sitting on the board there, I'm just anxious to get in the water and get wet."

The photo—showing Mollie reclining on the diving board—was published in the *Maple Leaf*, the newspaper for Canadian troops. Mollie didn't know it, but her picture was distributed to hundreds of thousands of Canadian fighting men. Something about the photo hit home, especially for the units fighting their way through Italy. Mollie would become more popular there than Hollywood stars like Rita Hayworth or Betty Grable. "I think it was just the typical 'gal-next-door' from back home kind of picture," Mollie says. "I think maybe they got a little much of Betty Grable and all these gorgeous Hollywood stars and they wanted to remember something from home."

There was not much beauty in the lives of Canadian soldiers, and those who fought in Italy were no exception. The war in Italy was two years of hardship and horror. Canadian units battled their way north, village by village, suffering heavy casualties with every advance. It was no wonder they embraced Mollie's picture and everything it stood for: beauty, wholesomeness, and the Canadian way of life.

Mollie herself had no idea she was such a celebrity until she started receiving letters from servicemen overseas. Her husband was not very happy with all the attention. "He was very, very upset because we had not been married that long. And I suppose I would have felt the same way if my husband had been receiving letters from women that we didn't know from a hole in the ground. So they all went into the fireplace."

Ninety-three thousand Canadians served in Italy. Six thousand of them never made it home. But those who did return have Mollie to thank, at least in a small way. She gave them what they needed most, a reminder of why they were there and who they were fighting for and, most importantly, a reason to make it back alive.

The photo of Mollie in a bathing suit at poolside was published in the Maple Leaf, *the newspaper for Canadian troops.* MOLLIE HOUGH

City for a Day

～

"IT MADE US, THE KING AND I. IT CAME AT JUST THE RIGHT TIME." These were the words that the late Queen Elizabeth, the Queen Mother, used to describe her landmark 1939 tour of Canada with her husband, King George VI—and for good reason. Canadians had waited a long time for their first visit from a reigning British monarch. They came out in record numbers, if only to catch a passing glimpse of the king and queen, and nowhere more than in Saskatchewan. By the time the royals headed home, it was estimated that half a million people, or fifty-six percent of the provincial population, had seen the couple. The most amazing story was that of Melville, Saskatchewan, which went from small town to big city in one glorious day.

King George and Queen Elizabeth arrived in Quebec City on 17 May 1939 to begin a forty-six-day tour of Canada. It was the first real test for the royal couple, who had been unexpectedly thrust into their roles with the abdication of King Edward VIII only two years earlier. The trip was a success. The couple's easy, unassuming style, together with the adoring crowds, made the tour a resounding triumph that astounded even the royals themselves.

The royal couple travelled by train across the country to Victoria on the Canadian Pacific line and then returned to Halifax on the Canadian National line. On the westward leg of the journey, the King and Queen passed through southern Saskatchewan, briefly stopping at Regina and Moose Jaw on 25 May. The province had just endured ten long years of depression and drought, and on the eve of the royal visit it started to rain. The long-awaited break in the drought, coupled with the arrival of the King and Queen, seemed a sign of good things to come.

Despite the damp weather, nothing was going to prevent Saskatchewan's citizens from seeing the royal couple. At each stop, even at small towns along the rail line where the train was not expected to stop, huge crowds gathered. More than one hundred thousand people waited through light drizzle in Regina. Another forty

The local Pool elevator was painted in honour of the royal visit to Melville.
SASKATCHEWAN ARCHIVES BOARD R-A 15061

thousand braved a heavy downpour in Moose Jaw. The rain did not deter the royals either. They insisted that activities continue as planned, even going as far as to ask that the top be left down on their car as they made their way through the streets in each city.

On the return trip across Canada, the royal train followed the northerly route across the prairie parkland with stops in Saskatoon and Melville on 3 June. Melville, in east-central Saskatchewan, was named in honour of Charles Melville Hays, president of the Grand Trunk Pacific Railway who had died in the 1912 sinking of the *Titanic*. Although known as a railway town in 1939, Melville was also an agricultural service centre for a largely immigrant population.

Melville was one of the last western stops on the tour, and one of the last chances for people to see the couple. Farm families reportedly came from as far as two hundred miles away. Cars and trucks rolled in all day from all directions, including Manitoba and the northern United States. It would reportedly take three hours to clear the traffic jam. Special trains, meanwhile, brought groups from nearby towns; even boxcars were used in some instances. The towns of Yorkton, Canora, and Esterhazy simply closed for the day as all of their residents headed to Melville.

Melville had spent weeks preparing for the visit. A huge sign proclaiming "Welcome to Their Majesties" was painted on the side of the local Pool elevator. Although the elevator has since been torn down, a replica with the same wording is featured today in a display at the Canadian Museum of Civilization in Hull, Quebec.

Melville also held the biggest sports day in its history. The celebrations began early in the morning, even though the train was not scheduled to arrive until 10 PM. Horse races, track-and-field events, and a baseball tournament took place at a new sports ground developed especially for the royal visit.

The town's hotels, restaurants, and concessions were all busy, while beer parlours did a brisk business, thanks in no small part to the Melville town council. Worried that the festivities would have to be shut down at midnight because of Sunday laws, Melville switched to Mountain Standard Time for the day so that there could be an extra hour of celebration.

A parade featuring bands and floats from surrounding towns

began working its way along Melville's streets at 6 PM. Two hours later, the crowd, including six hundred Great War veterans and an estimated ten thousand school children, moved to the reception grounds at the train station, where a two-hundred-piece orchestra played.

Shortly after 10 PM, the royal train pulled into Melville's station to the roar of the crowd. Moments later, King George and Queen Elizabeth stepped into a blue spotlight to a thundering cheer. After a brief welcoming address, the couple moved to a special floodlit platform for introductions and further presentations.

Smiling and waving, but unable to see beyond the platform because of the spotlight, Queen Elizabeth asked that the light be passed over the audience. She and the king were stunned by the size of the crowd: there were an estimated sixty thousand people. In one day, Melville, with a usual population of four thousand, had become a city.

The couple briefly mingled with the crowd then returned to their train just twenty minutes after their arrival. As they waved from the back of the last car before disappearing inside, fireworks were set off. The train was originally scheduled to spend the night in Melville. But when the crowd refused to disperse, the train slowly started to pull away and the couple came out again to wave their final goodbyes. The train stopped a few miles away, where it stayed for the night before continuing eastward early the next morning.

There was no rest, though, for two reporters for the *Yorkton Enterprise*. While being driven back to Yorkton by car, one of the reporters developed photos in the back seat while the other got to work on the story; a special commemorative edition of the paper, complete with pictures, appeared only hours later.

Melville's extraordinary welcome made headline news across North America. Reporters were struck by how Melville's immigrant population, most from central and eastern Europe, had so eagerly embraced the visiting couple.

The scene also left a lasting impression on the royals. In a thank-you telegram to the town administrator the next day, King George confessed, "The Queen and I will not easily forget the scene which greeted us at Melville. We send our heartfelt thanks to your fellow citizens and to all those from the surrounding country who joined them in welcoming us last night."

King George VI and Queen Elizabeth were the first reigning British monarchs to visit Canada. SASKATCHEWAN ARCHIVES BOARD R-A 18946

The Melville celebrations did more than just boost the confidence of the royal couple; it also reassured British officials of Canadian loyalty to the Crown. Throughout the royal tour, there were regular dispatches about the deteriorating situation in Europe and the looming threat of another war. Naturally, British officials travelling with the royal couple wondered how Canadians would respond. The Melville stop left no doubt. The royal tour drummed up loyalty and devotion to England just weeks before the start of the Second World War. Thousands of Canadians would go on to give their lives to protect Britain and the Commonwealth, including many who were there on that extraordinary day in Melville.

Lions in Winter

〜

THEY WERE YOUNG, BRASH, AND VIRTUALLY UNKNOWN. FOUR MEN from Saskatchewan, relatively new to curling, represented the province at the 1959 Brier, the Canadian curling championship. The game would never be the same.

The Richardson brothers, originally from Stoughton, Saskatchewan, took up curling late by prairie standards. Sam and Ernie had already graduated from high school in Regina, when, on a whim, they joined a local curling club. Together with their cousins, they formed a team skipped by tall, lanky Ernie, who would become one of the most imposing figures in the game. Younger brother Garnet (nicknamed Sam) was second, cousin Arnold was third or vice-skip, and cousin Wes was lead.

"The very first year we had matching sweaters and slacks," recalls Sam, who has written a book about the famous rink. "We always tried to look sharp and look like a curling team, even though we weren't very good." But the team gradually improved. The four young men had a natural chemistry, playing the game as a tightly knit team. And it soon paid dividends.

In 1955, the Brier came to Regina, and the Richardsons were in the stands. Saskatchewan had never won the Canadian national curling championship, but the Campbell brothers of Avonlea swept to victory with a perfect 10-0 record. Sam turned to his mother and said, "We're going to play in the Brier some day."

Watching some of the best curlers in the country inspired the Richardsons. "After that, we got really serious about the game," Sam remembers. "We went to every little town bonspiel. It didn't matter if it was thirty below inside the rink or outside the rink. Four years later we went to the Brier."

The upstart Richardsons were a long shot. Curling was a different game in the 1950s. The ice was natural and unpredictable. The brooms were heavy and made of straw. Teams played a draw game—trying to keep rocks in play—and the scores were high. But the

Richardson rink changed that. They were systematic, competitive, but above all aggressive in removing their opponents' stones. In 1959, they won their first Brier.

One day after winning the national championship in Quebec City, the Richardsons were on their way to Scotland. Nineteen fifty-nine was the first year for an international playoff. The best teams from Canada and Scotland, the home of curling, would face each other on the ice for the Scotch Cup.

The members of the Willie Young rink did not know what hit them. The Scots played a gentlemanly draw game. They considered it unsportsmanlike to deliberately strike an opponent's rock. But the Richardsons had perfected a deadly game of aggressive take-outs and accurate draws to the button. They cleared stones away from the front of the rings and threw them through the house to retain the hammer.

"We were sweeping to hit and roll out and get the blank," Sam explained, "and we could hear the old Scottish fellows in the background say, 'Aye, that's not curling. It's not curling blanking the end.' They asked us, 'Why did you blank it?' And Ernie said, 'We blanked

The world champion Richardson rink (left to right: Ernie, Arnold, Garnet [Sam], and Wes) with Saskatchewan Premier Tommy Douglas.
SASKATCHEWAN ARCHIVES BOARD R-A11522

it because we try to score more than one. We don't play for one.'" The Richardson rink humiliated the Scots with five straight victories and returned to Regina as heroes.

They won the Brier and Scotch Cup again in 1960, but lost in the Brier final the following year. They were back with a vengeance in 1962 and won two more national and international championships.

Their record is still untouched. The Richardson rink is the only team to have won the Brier four times, and Ernie is the only skip named to the Order of Canada. "We changed the game from a draw game in '59 to more of a hitting game. More of a sweeping game," Sam proudly claimed. "You know, curling was always called the 'roaring game' and we had big sweeping noise and a big voice to go with it. We put the roar back in the roaring game."

The Richardson hitting style caught on and the game of curling was never the same again. It was an aggressive, low-scoring game. But it also proved boring. Spectators wanted more action on the ice, more points. Three decades later, curling rules were changed to limit take-outs and ensure that more rocks remained in play each end.

Death Over Moose Jaw

IN MARCH 1954, THE MAYOR OF MOOSE JAW WROTE THE COMMANDER at the local air base, complaining about the number of planes flying over the city. Citizens were worried that an accident in the skies could have tragic consequences on the ground. They were right.

Moose Jaw has been home to an air base since the Second World War. As part of the British Commonwealth Air Training Plan, which operated between 1940 and 1945, hundreds of young men came to Saskatchewan's third largest city to learn how to fly. The Royal Canadian Air Force reopened the base as a pilot training centre in 1952 and welcomed NATO forces in the following decades.

One of the first young student pilots to come to Moose Jaw in the 1950s was Thomas Thorrat from Scotland. At 9:57 AM on 8 April 1954 he took off from the base in his Harvard training jet into beautiful, clear, and sunny skies. It was supposed to be a routine solo flight over Moose Jaw.

As the jet gradually gained altitude, Thorrat may have been checking his instruments or his maps. He failed to notice the approach of a commercial North Star airliner from the east. A Trans-Canada Airlines plane was on a scheduled run from Montreal to Vancouver. It was cruising at six thousand feet above the city with thirty-five people aboard.

Six minutes after takeoff, still oblivious to the danger above, Thorrat flew directly into the path of the passenger plane, shearing off its right wing. The North Star exploded in mid-air and split into two. The front of the plane rotated end over end as it fell to earth. Witnesses who heard the impact of the collision described seeing bodies fall from the sky "like teardrops."

The tail of the North Star crashed into the home of Gordon and Betty Hume, setting off an explosion on the quiet residential street. Their house was completely demolished, while two nearby homes were set on fire. The only casualty on the ground was Mrs. Martha Hawden, a mother of three who worked as a cleaning lady in the

The tail section of the passenger plane demolished a Moose Jaw home, narrowly missing a nearby school full of children at the time. LEADER-POST COLLECTION, SASKATCHEWAN ARCHIVES BOARD R-LP7

Hume house. Less than half an hour before the crash, Betty Hume had left for a dental appointment, taking her two young daughters with her. Miraculously, a school less than one hundred yards away from the Hume home, with over three hundred students inside, was left untouched.

The bodies of the victims and the debris from the two planes were scattered over a seven-square-mile area. Firemen called to put out the fires encountered a gruesome scene—most of the corpses were headless.

Thorrat was found dead in the wreckage of his jet at the golf course. All thirty-five people aboard the North Star also died, including Rodney Adamson, a Progressive Conservative member of Parliament who had served in both world wars.

The Moose Jaw crash was Saskatchewan's worst air disaster and, up until that time, the worst air disaster in Canadian history. There was some speculation that the accident may have been caused by Thorrat deliberately and foolishly "buzzing" the airliner. In the end, though, investigators blamed the crash on human error.

The tragedy gave substance to local complaints about pilots flying over Moose Jaw and prompted changes in flight patterns. Some people even began to question the merits of having a training base so close to the city. But despite the crash of 1954, 15 Wing Moose Jaw remains an integral part of the city's identity as the home to the world-famous Snow Bird aerobatic group.

Factoria

IT WAS BILLED AS SASKATCHEWAN'S FIRST INDUSTRIAL PARK—FACTORIA. One newspaper ad suggested that it was the keystone to prosperity. Another claimed that the name meant money. But, like many boom-time schemes, it was built on a foundation of greed and gullibility.

The coming of hundreds of thousands of immigrant farmers to western Canada in the first decade of the twentieth century sparked a dramatic growth in urban centres to serve the agricultural population. Villages appeared almost overnight, while towns and cities vied with one another for regional dominance.

The story of Saskatoon, known at the time as the Wonder City, was particularly spectacular. To say it boomed is an understatement. It grew from a hamlet of 113 in 1901 to a city of 12,000 in just ten years. Even then, Saskatoon boosters disputed the 1911 census figures and conducted their own headcount, including people staying in hotels or passing through on trains.

Part of Saskatoon's remarkable growth was attributable to the three major railways that ran through the city by 1908, hence its other nickname, "Hub City." It also secured the provincial university in 1909. The most important ingredient in Saskatoon's growth, however, was the unbridled optimism of the period: real estate boomed.

Between 1910 and 1913, real estate agents sold the equivalent of three Saskatoons of the size of the one that exists today. Over sixty subdivisions went on the market during the three-year period. Most were never developed. In all, fifteen thousand acres were surveyed outside the city limits in 1911—enough land to accommodate an estimated population of five hundred thousand people, half the population of Saskatchewan today.

Factoria had its beginnings in 1909 when Billy Silverwood, a local livestock dealer, purchased land just north of Saskatoon and built a huge barn to support his livery stable business. Silverwood discovered that his land had a natural spring, and he began to bottle the water and sell it in the city to people unwilling to drink from the

Saskatoon, The Wonder City. LOCAL HISTORY ROOM, SASKATOON PUBLIC LIBRARY

sewage-polluted South Saskatchewan River. His Silverwood Springs plant sold an estimated 120,000 bottles of water a year.

Silverwood's spring attracted the attention of R. E. Glass, a Chicago businessman and promoter who was looking for a good source of water for a brewery. He bought the Silverwood farm in 1912, and announced that the site would soon be the home of a new industrial city called Factoria. Glass predicted that all kinds of businesses would want to be part of the great venture.

Claiming that industry was the key to Saskatoon's future growth, Glass began to sell lots for five hundred dollars each. He also ran full- and half-page ads in the local newspapers every day for six months, extolling Factoria's investment potential. Factoria's future, in Glass's words, was "absolutely assured."

Several companies were won over by Glass's promotional efforts. And why not, given the boom that Saskatoon was experiencing? By 1913, the site boasted a flour plant, a sawmill, an implement manufacturer, two brick factories, and a hotel. But a recession swept across western Canada in the fall of 1913. The coming of war a year later only confirmed what many refused to admit—that the boom was over, and with it the great hopes for Factoria.

Glass never built his brewery; hundreds of people lost their money on lots that were never developed. Even the spring fell into disuse when the city built a water treatment system.

Today, the name Factoria has disappeared from the map. But Silverwood hasn't. It's the name of a neighbourhood in north Saskatoon. The city did eventually reach Billy Silverwood's land, seventy years too late for the people who invested in Factoria.

The Price of Pride

THE GREAT DEPRESSION HIT SASKATCHEWAN HARDER THAN ANY OTHER province in Canada. It was a desperate time, and people responded with desperate measures—none more so than Ted and Rose Bates.

British immigrants Ted and Rose Bates owned the butcher shop in Glidden, Saskatchewan, just south of Kindersley. Through the late 1920s, they ran a successful business and raised their only son, Jackie. Harry McDonald, Jackie's pal and the son of the town grocer, remembers Ted as a jolly, outgoing man. Rose was quite the opposite: quiet and reserved. Life was good for the Bates—but that all would change.

The Depression crippled Glidden. Record low wheat prices, combined with unrelenting drought, devastated the region's farm economy and left thousands struggling to survive. Many people living in rural areas had to turn to government assistance to get through the worst years of the decade. Glidden residents could barely afford groceries, much less the meat that Ted sold. The Bates were forced to close their shop in 1932. They decided to move west to try their luck in Vancouver, and opened another butcher shop there. But after only a year, the new business failed as well.

By 1933, the country had reached the low point of the Depression. The unemployment rate hit a staggering thirty per cent. More than a million people were living on some kind of government relief. Millions more refused to take it, too proud to go on the dole. The Bates had no choice, though. Having lost everything for a second time, they swallowed their pride and applied for relief. But they were turned down because they were not Vancouver citizens. They were told that they could collect relief only in their hometown. They had to return to Saskatchewan.

Rose was devastated. She told a friend, "I'd rather kill myself than go back to Glidden." Ted was equally distraught. "He looked to me like a man blown up by a shell, buried and blown up again," a friend remembered. But back they went.

In November 1933, thanks to assistance from the Salvation Army,

Jackie Bates (left) and Harry McDonald were childhood friends in Glidden. H. MCDONALD

they arrived in Saskatoon by train and applied for relief. But again, they were turned down. They had to return to Glidden.

Too proud to go home, and with nowhere else to turn, they hatched a desperate plan. While in Saskatoon, Rose sold her rings and some other belongings. With the money, they rented a car. They headed west on 4 December, toward Glidden but with no intention of ever getting there.

At nightfall, Ted pulled into the isolated Avalon schoolyard, near Biggar. The family of three got into the back seat and snuggled up under blankets to stay warm. They left the car running, confident that the carbon monoxide would kill them in their sleep. But sometime during the night, the car ran out of gas: they had not been able to afford a full tank. Rose woke and called to Ted who was groggy and sick from the car exhaust. Jack lay between them—dead.

Distraught, Rose begged Ted to kill her. He tried knocking her out with the engine crank, but didn't have enough strength. He then slashed at her neck with a penknife. Finally, he took a razor and cut his own wrists. Once again, they waited for death to take them.

In the morning, a farmer spotted the car and looked inside. It was a sight beyond horror. He frantically called the police.

Despite all that they had done, Ted and Rose were still alive. The couple were taken to hospital in Biggar, where they told the police their story. The RCMP charged them with murdering their son. Rose is rumoured to have said, "I know we'll hang and we'll deserve it."

Eight-year-old Jackie was buried a few days later in the Glidden cemetery. His funeral packed the community hall. Harry McDonald still remembers it. "We marched around the coffin, an open casket… and I can remember very distinctly to this very day, Jackie Bates died of carbon monoxide poisoning and you could see it in his face. You know what that entails … there's a bluish look to the lips."

Ted and Rose, in the meantime, were awaiting trial. But they did not face the court's justice alone. The people of Glidden, the very people they had been too ashamed to face, rallied to their defence by raising money and hiring a high-profile Saskatoon lawyer, Harry Ludgate.

"Everybody's heart went out to them. My dad was one of the people that collected money," recalls McDonald. "Maybe they didn't feel it, but the town held hands out to them."

The community refused to abandon Ted and Rose. Instead, they blamed the tragedy on the Depression and the failure of the government to do more to help the unfortunate family.

The couple went on trial in Wilkie in the spring of 1934. Their lawyer raised doubts about how young Jackie had died. Was it carbon monoxide poisoning? Or was it the weakened heart that he had been born with?

The jury reached a verdict in two hours. Not guilty.

Ted and Rose tried to rebuild their shattered lives. They moved to Rosetown, where Ted worked as a butcher until his death in 1954. Rose then returned to her family in England. But people say they were never the same without their little Jackie.

An Unlikely Spy

~

IN THE 1920s, COMMUNISM WAS VIEWED AS A VERY REAL THREAT TO the Canadian way of life. Saskatchewan, with its immigrant population from Eastern Europe, was considered a potential hotbed for subversive groups. One man would be given the job of infiltrating those groups and saving the good people of Canada from the Red Menace: John Leopold, an unlikely spy. By day, Leopold was a simple house painter. But by night, he worked as a spy for the Royal Canadian Mounted Police.

The 1920s were tumultuous political times. The Russian Revolution had just ended and western countries were paranoid that the Reds were everywhere. Canada's world-renowned police force resorted to cloak-and-dagger tactics to infiltrate the Communist forces. Leopold was one of their recruits.

Not much is known about Leopold. Many of his records are still sealed by the federal government. More than half a century after his assignment, the information is apparently still deemed too sensitive to be released. What is known is that Leopold was born in Bohemia (in the present-day Czech Republic). He came to Canada in 1912 and tried homesteading in Northern Alberta. But he failed as a farmer, and applied to join the RCMP. His foreign accent and appearance, combined with his ability to speak several languages, interested the Mounties. They knew he would be the perfect man to go undercover amongst immigrant and radical labour groups, the two groups the Mounties were targeting in their search for Communists. Most members of the force at that time were white, Anglo-Saxon Protestants. They would have stuck out like sore thumbs if they had tried infiltrating either of these groups.

Leopold fit right into the Mounties' plan, but he also presented problems. For starters, he stood four inches short of the force's required height. He also had a drinking problem. But the RCMP didn't let these details deter them. Leopold was accepted, trained, and posted to Regina in 1919. There, he assumed the identity of Jack

John Leopold (second row, far right) did not meet the minimum height requirement for a mountie. NATIONAL ARCHIVES OF CANADA PA202134

Esselwein, house painter. Over the next nine years, Number 30—his code name—became active in various radical labour organizations. He even helped organize a local branch of the Communist Party of Canada (CPC). He became secretary of the local CPC branch. Through the entire time, Leopold reported regularly to his superiors. He kept his files in a room he rented at a house owned by a Mountie colleague.

But Leopold's double life began taking its toll. He lived in constant fear that he would be exposed, and possibly harmed. It was a fear that was with him twenty-four hours a day for almost ten years. He also found life as an undercover agent to be lonely and began to drink excessively. He even claimed his liquor purchases on his RCMP expense account.

He finally made the kind of mistake he and his superiors had been dreading. He put his shoes up on a table at a party, revealing the RCMP imprint on the soles. Leopold claimed that he had purchased them at a second hand store. But the incident aroused suspicion, and Leopold's cover was soon blown.

Leopold's fear of violent reprisal turned out to be unfounded. The Communist Party simply expelled him in 1928. He was re-assigned to the Yukon where he was forced into uniform for the first time. But his knowledge of Communist groups eventually landed him a job in the intelligence service in Ottawa in 1935, where he served as an expert in Communism.

John Leopold's career as a spy was only the beginning of the RCMP's undercover activities. The force had agents and informants working in Canada right up until the 1970s at all kinds of subversive places, including university campuses across western Canada. Now the job of domestic intelligence gathering belongs to the Canadian Security Intelligence Service, which was founded in 1984.

An Epidemic of Bullets

◡

THE ELK THAT ROAM PRINCE ALBERT NATIONAL PARK ARE SUPPOSED to be protected, but it hasn't always been that way. In 1959, elk conservation took a back seat to the political goals of the prime minister at the time, John G. Diefenbaker.

The fall of 1959 was extremely wet in the area north of Prince Albert. Farmers had to leave their unharvested crops in the field. For the elk that made Prince Albert National Park their home, it was like an all-you-can-eat buffet right outside the park boundaries. The farmers generally viewed the damage done by elk to their crops with a certain degree of resignation. But this year the presence of elk was unacceptable. Farmers were afraid the elk would eat all of the crops, leaving nothing for a late harvest.

As a park warden, Cliff Millard watched over Prince Albert National Park for forty-one years. He was not surprised when farmers in the area started complaining to Ottawa about the elk. "We knew that the elk were going out and bothering the farmers' crops," he remembers. "They were getting into the wheat fields and the swaths. Making a mess."

The secretary of the Rural Municipality of Shellbrook wrote to the area's member of Parliament, Progressive Conservative John Diefenbaker. He explained the problem and asked that farmers be compensated and that steps be taken to prevent future crop damage. He even wondered whether a fence along the southern park boundary might be the answer. The response he received was extreme and entirely unexpected.

John Diefenbaker was not only the representative for the Prince Albert riding; he also happened to be Prime Minister of Canada. On 14 December 1959, he ordered the elk problem to be dealt with "promptly and efficiently." No one was quite sure what that meant, until forty-eight hours later, when Cliff Millard and his fellow wardens got their orders. "The chief warden phoned up and said we're going elk hunting," Millard recalls. "We were told to start shooting."

Prince Albert National Park Warden Emmett Millard (front, second from right) suddenly developed terrible aim during the elk extermination program. R. HUBEL

Diefenbaker had signed off on a wholesale slaughter. The park wardens were ordered to kill elk. There was no limit, and every animal was considered a target, even pregnant ones, and females with young. Any elk caught outside the park boundaries was considered free game for civilian hunters. To counter any suggestion that the plan was politically motivated, the government issued a press release stating the program was intended to reduce herds to the carrying capacity of the park.

It was a winter-long slaughter. When the guns finally fell silent on 6 March 1960, more than four hundred elk were dead. The herd was decimated and the wardens were devastated. "It went against the grain of all park wardens to be shooting off our elk," says Cliff Millard. "It should have never happened. But the only ones who could do the shooting were the wardens. We were told to go and do it, so we had to go ahead."

But not everyone went ahead. Millard's uncle Emmett was also a park warden, one with a soft spot for the park animals. Normally a good shot, he suddenly developed terrible aim. According to Millard, "He done a lot of shooting, but never hit anything. Of course he loved elk."

No one knows for sure why Diefenbaker ordered the slaughter. The government had other options, such as fencing off the southern edge of the park or reimbursing farmers for lost crops. But if it was votes the prime minister was after, he got them. Diefenbaker was re-elected in the riding for the next two decades.

Of course, this happened long before terms like environment or conservation became household words. The elk herd eventually recovered. But the slaughter left a lasting impression on those who were forced to do the shooting, the ones who had dedicated their careers to protecting the elk: the wardens of the Prince Albert National Park.

Damn Dam

IT WAS SUPPOSED TO BE SASKATCHEWAN'S HYDROELECTRIC PROJECT of the century. The La Colle Falls dam should have put Prince Albert on the map. Instead, it put the city in the poorhouse.

Founded in 1866 near the forks of the North and South Saskatchewan Rivers, Prince Albert—named in honour of Queen Victoria's consort—seemed destined for greatness. Within ten years, it was a thriving agricultural centre. The city was expected to continue to grow and prosper with the arrival of the Canadian Pacific Railway. But the railway never came. In 1881, in one of the most controversial decisions in western Canadian history, the proposed route along the North Saskatchewan River was abandoned in favour of sending the rail line across the southern prairies. The once great hopes of Prince Albert were never realized. The city that at one time expected to surpass Winnipeg in stature was reduced almost overnight to an economic backwater.

Prince Albert's fortunes, however, seemed to turn around in the early twentieth century. Like many other prairie centres during the so-called Laurier boom (1896–1911), the city experienced phenomenal growth. The 1911 population of nine thousand was double that of five years earlier. New services and new businesses flourished. The resources of the nearby forest, especially lumber and fish, were exploited at record levels. The city's potential was unlimited, or at least it seemed that way.

A blinkered optimism born of progress lay behind Prince Albert's dream to develop La Colle Falls. Located about twenty-five miles east of the city on the North Saskatchewan River, the falls were really little more than rapids. But in 1905, civic leaders looked to them as a source of cheap electric power. They believed the falls, once harnessed, would make the city the power-producing capital of western Canada, and in the process attract all kinds of business. The plan seemed a sure ticket to wealth and prestige.

After calling for engineering drawings and estimates, Prince Albert decided to proceed with the hydroelectric project. It would be the first power dam on the Canadian prairies. The project, featuring a 750-foot long dam and a 120-by-75-foot navigation lock, was to be built in three stages. Initial development, at a cost in excess of four hundred thousand dollars, would provide twenty-seven hundred horsepower. But if fully developed, the project could provide ninety-two hundred horsepower.

Questions should have been asked. No one seemed to be concerned that the local power market in 1909 consumed only six hundred horsepower, that the flow of the river in winter might not be enough to power the turbines, or that the federal government chose not to invest in the project. It did not matter. Prince Albert saw its future as the "White Coal" city, and a three-hundred-name petition in 1910 urged the city to embark on the project as soon as financing was in place.

Construction finally started in late April 1912, when the city signed a contract for the construction of the dam, lock, and intake works. The delay had done nothing to dampen Prince Albert's enthusiasm for the project. In fact, the city decided to build the project all at once. It also decided to finance the project entirely on its own. The price tag was $1.2 million, a staggering amount in 1912.

By September, over three hundred men were working at the site, while a small army of suppliers transported materials, equipment and food by water or road between Prince Albert and the falls. Most of the initial construction was confined to the dam and navigation lock on the south shore of the river. By the spring of 1913, the city let contracts for the excavation of the powerhouse and canal. On 4 June 1913, the gates for the lock were ordered. Prince Albert expected the dam to be finished in four to five months.

Then things turned sour. Because of a recession, Prince Albert had difficulty finding buyers for the power bonds to finance the project. Bills went unpaid, and a work slowdown was ordered on 11 July 1913. The project also lost large sums of money because of pilfering. There was no control over what supplies left Prince Albert and what arrived at La Colle.

The end came on 29 July when the Imperial Bank turned down a loan for two hundred thousand dollars. Work on the project stopped the same day. The dam extended 293 feet from the south bank of the river, leaving a 462-foot gap. Most of the other features, located on the north bank, including a canal intake and powerhouse, were only half-completed.

Despite the downturn, Prince Albert remained hopeful and tried to revive the project the following summer. But the economy remained in the doldrums, and Prince Albert's debt climbed. So, too, did the cost of the project. It was estimated it would now take a whopping $1.8 million to finish the project.

Prince Albert scrambled to keep the project alive during the First World War by offering to sell power to Saskatoon. It also tried to get the federal government involved. Both efforts were unsuccessful.

By 1918, the reality of Prince Albert's folly could no longer be ignored. Even the prospect of river traffic actually using the lock evaporated when steamboat service on the North Saskatchewan came to an end in 1919. When all the bills were added up, the outstanding cost of the discontinued project was over a million dollars. Without any other financial resources or credit to draw upon, Prince Albert

Construction of the dam and lock got underway in April 1912; the 1.2 million-dollar project was to be completed by the fall of 1914.
SASKATCHEWAN ARCHIVES BOARD R-A1796-2

went bankrupt. It was the first Saskatchewan city to default on its debt. The city's services had suffered greatly during the project. The attempt to keep the dam going took money away from other areas, such as water mains, sewage disposal, fire equipment, and even a new hospital. It would be years before these services and facilities could be upgraded.

Today, the long-abandoned dam reaches halfway across the North Saskatchewan River. Cement bags lie hardened where they were unloaded and stacked almost a century ago, while graffiti artists have left their mark on the walls of the half-finished navigation lock. It's a constant reminder of what false optimism can cost—as if the people of Prince Albert needed one. City taxpayers did not finish paying off the La Colle Falls project until 1965.

Sitting Bull's Mountie

~

IN MAY 1877, AMERICA'S MOST WANTED FUGITIVE FLED TO WOOD Mountain in southern Saskatchewan. Lakota Sioux chief Sitting Bull and his people were looking for sanctuary from the American government. And they got it—from an unlikely source.

In opening the American West to settlement, the United States waged war on the First Nations of the region. The American government spent more money fighting Indians in 1870 than the entire Canadian federal budget for that year. These battles between the U.S. Army and the First Nations of the plains reached a climax in June 1876, when General George Armstrong Custer attacked a large Sioux and Cheyenne village on the banks of the Big Horn River in southern Montana. The Sioux, led by Sitting Bull, easily routed the American cavalry, wiping out Custer and more than two hundred of his men. When news of the massacre reached the outside world, Sitting Bull became the most famous and most feared chief in North America.

After Little Big Horn, the Sioux became refugees in their own country. They knew that other First Nations groups had found sanctuary in Canada and decided to head north across the international border, or "Medicine Line," where they would come under the protection of Queen Victoria, known as the Great White Mother.

"Sitting Bull knew that there was going to be more soldiers coming after him," explained Leonard Lethbridge, a descendant of the Montana Sioux now living in Saskatchewan. "So he decided to come to Canada."

"He was a medicine man," added his cousin, Lawrence. "So they all kind of looked up to a medicine man."

The first group of Sioux reached the Wood Mountain region before Christmas 1876. By May, Sitting Bull had arrived with about one thousand followers. The area's Sioux population would eventually swell to five thousand by the end of the decade.

The Canadian government was not happy with the presence of the Sioux refugees. Officials were worried that Sitting Bull's presence might provoke intertribal warfare or worse, trouble with settlers. They also feared an international incident, especially with the Sioux so close to the border. Ottawa consequently assigned Major James Morrow Walsh of the North-West Mounted Police the job of keeping an eye on the unwanted visitors.

Walsh was one of the original officers of the NWMP and a natural leader; his men revered him. When he received his order he was commanding B Troop in the Cypress Hills. Upon hearing that Sitting Bull had crossed into Canada, Walsh headed to Wood Mountain and with only a handful of men rode into the famous chief's camp.

Walsh told Sitting Bull that his people were safe in Canada as long as they behaved. He also warned against raids and explained that Canada's laws applied to all equally. Then he issued hunting ammunition to the Sioux.

This first meeting was the beginning of a close and enduring friendship. In fact, Walsh spent so much time with the Sioux chief over the next few months that he came to be called "Sitting Bull's Mountie." He even moved the headquarters of B Troop to Wood Mountain so that they could be closer.

Sitting Bull appreciated the policeman's candour and honesty and looked to him for advice and protection. "Because Sitting Bull was a good judge of individuals, he knew that Walsh spoke with straight eyes," said Leonard. "He was truthful and Sitting Bull . . . trusted him." Walsh, in turn, realized that the old warrior's fighting days were over and that he wanted to live in peace. The Mountie supported the Sioux in every way he could, but he could do little about the new enemy of the Sioux—hunger.

"At the start it was not too bad," said Lawrence. "There was still some game left. But eventually it was all gone and they were starving to death. They had to eat their horses at the end before they went back to the States."

As game in the region became scarce and buffalo could no longer be found north of the border, hundreds of Sioux began slipping back to the United States. Walsh helped those who remained, even though it was against Ottawa's instructions to provide rations. In May 1880, Sitting Bull appealed to Walsh to help secure a permanent home in Canada for his starving people. But Walsh's request for a reserve only

Following the Battle of the Little Big Horn, Lakota Sioux Chief Sitting Bull became the most famous and most feared Indian in North America.

NWMP Major James Walsh was sent to Wood Mountain to watch over Sitting Bull and ensure that there was no trouble on Canadian soil.

angered the government, which pushed the NWMP to encourage the Sioux to return home.

"Sitting Bull was pretty inspirational," Leonard remarked, "and the Canadian government didn't like a charismatic person like that ... especially an Indian."

The Canadian government soon decided that Walsh was the problem and transferred him to Fort Qu'Appelle. Walsh ignored the order as long as he could, but was forced to leave on 15 July 1880. It would be the last time that Walsh and his friend Sitting Bull saw each other.

Sitting Bull remained in Canada for another year, but starvation eventually forced him to surrender to American authorities in North Dakota in July 1881. Walsh was powerless to help. Upset and disillusioned by how the great chief had been treated, he resigned from the NWMP in 1883.

Sitting Bull took up residence on the Standing Rock reservation and tried to settle down to a quiet life. But he could not find the peace he sought, and was killed there in 1890 trying to resist arrest.

Not all the Wood Mountain Sioux returned to the United States with Sitting Bull. Some, like the ancestors of Leonard and Lawrence Lethbridge, stayed behind and finally secured a reserve in 1917, finding the sanctuary that Sitting Bull had been seeking.

Further Reading

Abrams, Gary. *Prince Albert: The First Century, 1866–1966.* Saskatoon: Modern Press, 1976

Bagnell, K. *The Little Immigrants: The Orphans Who Came to Canada.* Toronto: Macmillan, 1980.

Barnhart, G. L. *Peace, Progress and Prosperity: A Biography of Saskatchewan's First Premier, T. Walter Scott.* Regina: Canadian Plains Research Centre, 2000.

Berton, Pierre. *The Great Depression, 1929–1939.* Toronto: McClelland & Stewart, 1990.

Brennan, J. W. *Regina: An Illustrated History.* Toronto: Lorimer, 1989.

Gray, James, *The Winter Years.* Toronto: Macmillan, 1966; Calgary: Fifth House Ltd., 2003.

Guitard, Michelle. "La Rolanderie." *Saskatchewan History* 30, no. 3 (1977): 110–14.

Hewitt, S. R. "Royal Canadian Police Spy; The Secret Life of John Leopold/Jack Esselwein." *Intelligence and National Security* 15, no.1 (2000): 144–68.

Hanson, Stan D. "Estevan 1931," in *On Strike: Six Key Labour Struggles in Canada,* edited by Irving Abella. Toronto: Lorimer, 1974.

Kalmakoff, Elizabeth. "Women in Saskatchewan Politics, 1916–1919." *Saskatchewan History* 46, no. 2 (1994): 3–18.

Kerr, Don and Stan D. Hanson. *Saskatoon: The First Half-Century.* Edmonton: NeWest, 1982.

Knuttila, Murray. *That Man Partridge: E.A. Partridge, His Thoughts and Times.* Regina: Canadian Plains Research Centre, 1994.

Larsen, John and Marice R. Libby. *Moose Jaw: People, Places, History.* Regina: Coteau, 2001.

Lux, Maureen K. "The Bitter Flats: The 1918 Influenza Epidemic in Saskatchewan." *Saskatchewan History* 49, no. 1 (1997): 3–14.

Millar, R. "Will James a.k.a. Ernest Dufault." *Saskatchewan History* 53, no. 1 (2001): 39–44.

Palmer, Howard. *Patterns of Prejudice.* Toronto: McClelland & Stewart, 1982.

Ransom, Diane. "The Saskatoon Lily: A Biography of Ethel Catherwood." *Saskatchewan History* 43, no. 3 (1988): 81–98.

Shepard, R. Bruce *Deemed Unsuitable.* Toronto: Umbrella, 1997.

Smith, David B. *Curling: An Illustrated History.* Edinburgh: Prometheus Books, 1981.

Stonechild, Blair and Bill Waiser. *Loyal till Death: Indians and the North-West Rebellion.* Calgary: Fifth House Ltd., 1997.

Tracie, Carl. *Toil and Peaceful Life: Doukhobor Village Settlement in Saskatchewan, 1899–1918.* Regina: Canadian Plains Research Centre, 1996.

Turner, C. Frank. *Across the Medicine Line.* Toronto: McClelland & Stewart, 1973.

Virtual Saskatchewan on-line magazine: www.virtualsk.com.

Waiser, Bill. *The New Northwest: The Photographs of the Frank Crean Expeditions, 1908–1909.* Saskatoon: Fifth House Ltd., 1993.

Waiser, Bill. *Saskatchewan's Playground: A History of Prince Albert National Park.* Saskatoon: Fifth House Ltd., 1989.

Walker, James. *Race, Rights and the Law in the Supreme Court of Canada: Historical Case Studies.* Waterloo: Osgoode Society for Canadian Legal History/Wilfrid Laurier University Press 1997.

Index

By Place

By Subject

COVER PHOTOGRAPHS

Front cover: *(top)* The French Counts of Whitewood (SASKATCHEWAN ARCHIVES BOARD R-B12483); *(left to right)* The Regina Cyclone (SASKATCHEWAN ARCHIVES BOARD R-B3778-10), Sitting Bull (SASKATCHEWAN ARCHIVES BOARD R-A8660), The Blizzard of '47 (SASKATCHEWAN ARCHIVES BOARD R-A 27895), The Saskatoon Lily, Ethel Catherwood (SASKATOON PUBLIC LIBRARY, LOCAL HISTORY ROOM LH3475)
Back cover: Edouard Beaupré, the Willow Bunch Giant (SASKATCHEWAN ARCHIVES BOARD R-A3465).

FIFTH HOUSE

About Fifth House Books

ifth House Publishers, a Fitzhenry & Whiteside company, is a proudly western-Canadian press. Our publishing specialty is non-fiction as we believe that every community must possess a positive understanding of its worth and place if it is to remain vital and progressive. Fifth House is committed to "bringing the West to the rest" by publishing approximately twenty books a year about the land and people who make this region unique. Our books are selected for their quality, saleability, and contribution to the understanding of Western Canadian (and Canadian) history, culture, and environment.

Look for these other books about Saskatchewan from Fifth House at your favourite bookstore.

Aunt Mary in the Granary and Other Prairie Stories,
    Eileen Comstock, $14.95
Buffalo Days and Nights, Peter Erasmus, $14.95
But It's a Dry Cold! Weathering the Canadian Prairies,
    Elaine Wheaton, $18.95
The Good Land: Stories of Saskatchewan People, Peter Wilson, $14.95
Inside Out: The Autobiography of a Native Canadian, James Tyman, $7.95
Just Another Indian: A Serial Killer and Canada's Indifference,
    Warren Goulding, $22.95
The Last Roundup: Memories of a Canadian Cowboy, Stan Graber, $12.95
Looking West: Photographing the Canadian Prairies, 1858–1957,
    Brock V. Silversides, $24.95
Loyal till Death: Indians and the North-West Rebellion, Blair Stonechild
    and Bill Waiser, $19.95
The Middle of Nowhere: Rediscovering Saskatchewan,
    Dennis Gruending, $16.95
No Spring Chicken: Thoughts on a Life Well Lived,
    Eileen Comstock, $16.95
Saskatchewan in Sight, John L. Perret, $34.95
SaskScandal: The Death of Political Idealism in Saskatchewan,
    Gerry Jones, $14.95
The Silent Song: A Tribute to a Reluctant Pioneer Mother,
    Marjorie Wilkins Campbell, $14.95
What's in a Name: The Story of Saskatchewan Place Names,
    E.T. Russell, $14.95
*Where the River Runs: Stories of the Saskatchewan and the People
    Drawn to Its Shores,* Victor Carl Friesen, $21.95